The life of Marie Younkin-Waldman who suffered progressive hearing loss from birth and was finally blessed with the modern miracle of a cochlear implant will tear at your heartstrings. Her mother's caring advocacy coupled with Marie's superior intelligence and generous heart provides inspiration and hope for those who struggle with any type of disability.

——**Alice Mott Huggins** Former "Miss Alice" on network television

After more than six decades of enduring life in a cocoon of near-silence, the author's hearing is miraculously awakened by a successful cochlear implant. What a treat to share her profound joy and gratitude as she gradually begins to recognize the infinite variety of sounds that most of us take for granted. This engaging, true story is related with warmth, openness and humility.

——**Louise McLeod** freelance editor

Marie has touchingly taken us on a journey from her beginnings as a child with progressive hearing loss through her coping strategies in adolescence and beyond culminating in her wonderful cochlear implant operation two years ago which enabled her to hear. Marie's journey is inspirational; I highly recommend this book.

——**Joan McMaster,** Chairperson
American Association of University Women
Annual Authors Luncheon (RI)

It has been a privilege to be a part of Marie's cochlear implant journey. Her story of perseverance and courage is an inspiration to all who seek personal fulfillment in spite of life's many challenges.

——**Eva Bero, AuD CCC-A**, Audiologist
Clinical Coordinator, Sounds of Life; Cochlear Implant Program
UMass Memorial Healthcare

Marie's book makes me appreciate once more the extraordinary graces in the midst of the ordinary round of affairs of a day. In a time of anxious uncertainty, reading these reflections serve as a tonic for despair over life's vicissitudes, and give hope and "good news" for a world hungry for the same!

——**The Rev. Craig Burlington,** Episcopal priest, St. Luke's Church
East Greenwich, RI

Marie Younkin-Waldman was an inspiration to many when she was profoundly deaf. Parenting, traveling, writing, hosting a tv talk show, she was a poster-woman for successfully living with a disability. Her vivid description of the miseries of a non-hearing adolescence and the depression she felt as she struggled to understand others show the cost of "doing it all." Her successful cochlear implant not only allowed her to hear music, talk radio and the voices of her grandchildren, but it also revived happy memories of the past through the simple songs of birds. Her story is an inspiration to anyone contemplating a major change in their lives.

——**Jane Lancaster, PhD**, author *Making Time: Lillian Moller Gilbreth — A Life Beyond …*

What a well-chosen title for Marie Younkin-Waldman's memoir, *To Hear the Birds Sing*. Not only is this a book about overcoming the many obstacles of a person growing up with hearing loss, but also as Marie so eloquently stated, " Hearing is knowing someone is behind you when they say "Good Morning."... It is having more opportunities." Marie explains about her opportunities after her cochlear implant with sensitivity and style.

——**Denise Carlson**, Program Coordinator: Adaptive Telephone Equipment Loan Program, RI

To Hear the Birds Sing is a heart warming memoir of a woman's journey and struggle with hearing loss from childhood. It's a journey of finding herself and the beauty all around her. Marie draws the reader in through her honest sharing of feelings, her humor and weaving her stories of going to school in France. A delightful book that will touch your heart and make you smile. A must read for anyone who seeks courage and hope.

——**Pat Hastings,** author *Simply a Woman of Faith*

A lovely story — a happy ending. Because of Marie's mother's care she decided to have the cochlear implant and now she can hear, even the birds in her garden. Those of us born to hear should never complain, even about the noises of this world, always on the move.

——**Monica Hickey** Legendary Bridal Director at Henri Bendel and Bergdorf Goodman

Marie is a breath of fresh air. In fact, in South County, Rhode Island, Marie is truly a strong breeze of optimism and beauty. Every page of this book reflects Marie's spirit which is bright and positive. This is a story that will move your spirit and bring tears to your eyes.

——**Rev. Betty Kornitzer**
Unitarian Universalist Congregation of South County, RI

Marie Younkin-Waldman is truly an inspirational writer, television show personality and caring human being. This book recounts her odyssey from progressive childhood hearing loss to her bold decision to have a cochlear implant. She shares her intense emotions as she regains hearing and experiences the delicious sounds of life: children's voices, bird calls, music and the sound of her own singing. *To Hear the Birds Sing: Conversations with My Heart* is a motivating read for everyone who longs for a sweet dose of aesthetics, nostalgia and courage.

——**Michael E. Gordon, PhD**
Dear friend and author *Trump University Entrepreneurship 101: How to Turn Your Idea into a Money Machine*

Marie Younkin-Waldman brings another heartfelt and important story our way with *To Hear the Birds Sing*. She so generously shares her story of what it's like to struggle in that "in between" world of hearing loss as child and then as an adult. ... This is an excellent book to help us understand how much more we lose when our hearing fails us. Few will take their hearing for granted after reading this book. Read it and share it with everyone you know!

——**Eileen Jones,** President & Founder
The Gift of Hearing Foundation

Although my own hearing loss was what prompted me to read *To Hear the Birds Sing*, I found myself fascinated by what an interesting life the author, Marie, has led. You do not need a hearing loss to enjoy this pleasant memoir.

——**Ann Scavone** Cochlear implant recipient

This book isn't just a celebration of modern magic. It is not merely a victory and a rediscovery. It is a poetic book with a sense of wonder and treasure.

——**Professor Mike Fink** Rhode Island School of Design

To Hear The Birds Sing

Conversations with my heart

Marie Younkin-Waldman

To: Ellie —
Hope you enjoy
the book —
Marie Younkin
Waldman

Gentility Press   Rhode Island, USA

Gentility Press

ALL RIGHTS RESERVED

The author and publisher have taken care in the preparation of
this book but make no expressed or implied warranty of any
kind and assume no responsibility for errors or omissions. No
liability is assumed for incidental or consequential damages in
connection with or arising out of the use of information
contained herein.

No part of this work may be reproduced, transmitted, stored,
or used in any form or by any means graphic, electronic, or
mechanical, photocopying, recording, or likewise, except as
permitted under Section 107 or 108 of the 1976 United States
Copyright Act, without the prior written permission of the
publisher. For information regarding permissions, write to:

Gentility Press
PO Box 3304
Narragansett, RI 02882

First Edition. First Printing: October, 2009
Copyright © 2009 by Marie Younkin-Waldman
ISBN 978-0-9747010-1-1

Printed in the United States of America
10 9 8 7 6 5 4 3 2 1

Acknowledgments

I would like to thank all those near and dear who suggested that I create a book after reading the email journal pages that I sent them about my implant experience.

Big thanks go to Betty Cotter, my editor and friend, who was a great help.

Thanks to my husband, Myron, for all of his technical knowledge and assistance with the cover and book design for this book as well as his continuous support.

Thanks to my special friends in my cochlear implant group: Eileen Jones, Ann Scavone and Peg Smith, and especially for their help during my implant procedure.

Thanks to my daughter, Dawne Galetta, who was with me during my implantation and has always been a big supporter of my writing.

I am grateful for the encouragement of my fellow writers in the writers' group at The Neighborhood Guild in Peace Dale, Rhode Island.

Thanks to the people who invented and perfected the cochlear implant.

Preface

Far too often, we are defined by what we can't do. For many years Marie Younkin-Waldman struggled to hear and every obstacle and triumph in her life was centered on this struggle. From a childhood with a domineering father and a loving, but overprotective mother, Marie strove to build an identity separate from her disability. She dropped out of college and married young, trading her privileged but sheltered upbringing for an uncertain and tumultuous marriage. Four children, difficult in-laws and an even more difficult first husband did not deter her from the fight for self - a fight to build a happy and fulfilling life despite the isolation brought on by her growing deafness.

When a cochlear implant in her right ear in 2007 re-connected Marie with sound, a door opened. But *To Hear the Birds Sing* - her moving account of this operation - is more than just another story of the triumph of technology. What is most interesting about the book is the author's determination to live a full life even after her activation at age 63. Through divorce, remarriage and career changes, and the evolution of a more public life, we witness a woman determined not to live a life of silence. Whether insisting on being heard or belting out Broad-way tunes, Marie Younkin-Waldman stands up for anyone who has been unable to participate fully in the world. This is ultimately not a story about processors and batteries but of a woman who would not be denied her place in life - who resolved to hear it all, noise and music, cacophony and melody, and who greeted those sounds with the unique song of her own self.

Betty J. Cotter
Author of *Roberta's Woods*
Wakefield, RI

Forward

Cochlear implants are marvelous bionic devices that provide sound and speech understanding to infants, children and adults of all ages who have severe to profound hearing loss. Our ability to provide hearing to deaf patients has evolved considerably since Alessandro Volta placed metal rods connected to a battery into his ears and heard a noise. The modern cochlear implant represents the culmination of many years of biomedical research, refinements in temporal bone surgery and the early perseverance of several groups of surgeons and scientists in the fields of otology, audiology and neuroscience. Current implant designs include a sophisticated microphone and speech processor that is worn externally on the ear to convert the analog signal of sound and speech to an electronic signal. The digital message is enhanced and then wirelessly transmitted to a surgically implanted receiver-stimulator whose multiple electrodes are delicately placed into the deaf cochlear. The cochlear implant represents the most successful attempt to restore a special sensory organ, bypassing the thousands of delicate hair cells of the inner ear to electrically stimulate the surviving auditory nerves. Even more remarkable, however, is the capacity of the human brain to decode the relatively crude signal generated by the implant to provide meaningful sound and speech abilities to the majority of users.

Marie Younkin-Waldman has committed her adult life to helping others- as a mother, a wife, a teacher, a therapist, a columnist and as host and producer of a popular cable television show. She has been actively involved for many years to advocate for those with hearing loss on both a local and national level. I first met Marie as a patient who had struggled for many years with her own progressive hearing loss. I was humbled by how well she managed to cope with her condition as well as her extraordinary energy and passion in her advocacy work for others. It has been a privilege for my cochlear implant team to provide Marie with the renewed ability to hear her family, friends and the world around her. Her story, "To Hear the Birds Sing," as well as the countless stories shared by our many cochlear implant patients and family members, are constant reminders of the remarkable plasticity of the brain and the resiliency of the human spirit.

Daniel J. Lee, M.D.
Department of Otology and Laryngology
Massachusetts Eye and Ear Infirmary
Harvard Medical School
Boston, Massachusetts

"Whatever you can do
or dream you can do.
Begin it.
Boldness has genius, power and magic in it."

Goethe

Table of Contents

1

In The Beginning

May 2007

W hen I came to, my daughter, Dawne, was sitting next to me. I felt great but was saying strange things to her such as how much I liked her husband, Dave, and my daughter-in-law, Sara. Like a drunken woman in a cloudy stupor I kept repeating what good spouses they were, something I had never expressed so openly to anyone. Suddenly, I needed to lie down again. I could feel the cold wet ice chips Dawne was spreading over my lips.

The nurse reattached the IV and busied herself at my other side. I started to succumb to the waves of nausea and fatigue that were flooding my body. It was May 11th, 2007, and I had just completed major surgery with Dr. Daniel Lee at UMass Memorial Hospital in Worcester, Massachusetts. Although I could hear nothing after he implanted the cochlear electrode device in my right ear, I was confident that I would be able to hear in a few weeks after the healing and recovery period when

I would be activated and fitted with a processor. Then I hoped to join the hearing world after a lifetime of progressive hearing loss and see how my life was going to change.

I was born in 1944 near the end of World War II, in Newport News, Virginia, when my father, Chief Petty Officer Adolph Neubert was stationed with the U.S. Navy. The umbilical cord was wrapped around my neck, leaving me with a bilateral progressive sensorineural hearing loss. In a way I was lucky. This kind of birth can leave children with further complications. I also had high fevers from early childhood diseases that could have contributed to my loss. The cause has never been completely determined by medical professionals. When I was growing up my loss was moderate and I was able to function fairly well. My mother, Martha Richey Neubert, lead the way for me with my teachers in elementary school to make sure I had what I needed. Mother also spent much time taking me to audiologists who tested me in soundproof booths. But, as I recall, nothing seemed to happen beyond that testing.

When I reached eighth grade in Maplewood Junior High School in New Jersey I used to come home every day crying. I cried because the boys who sat behind me put chewing gum in my hair. I couldn't hear their comments and teasing from behind (but I could feel the hurt). Adolescent angst probably added to the mix also. That was when I started to fall behind in math and music, not realizing at the time that those were cumulative information-gathering subjects based on what had previously been learned. When I could only hear things sporadically it was natural that I would not be able to keep up with that kind of learning. I did much better in Social Studies and English so I just figured that, like most girls then, I wasn't very good in math.

In ninth grade, my parents put me in a private girls' school, The Beard School, in Orange, New Jersey, which had small classes that prepared me for college. In fact, I was on the honor roll at Beard, proving that I could really learn. During my teen years, Mother took me to St. Barnabas Hospital in Newark to an intimidating psychologist, whom I hated. He stared down at me as he kept saying in a severe voice, "You must say out loud that you are deaf." I felt like crying and I may have. I had never heard of being deaf in my denial-focused home environment. It sounded terrible and surely I was not deaf. There were also speech classes with a pathologist and an audiologist to help me get fitted for a hearing aid. I hated wearing the aid, as I did not know anyone else my age who wore one. The aid caused sounds that seemed unnatural and it hurt my ears so I would not wear it. I guess no one encouraged me to wear it either. What a waste of years. Now I tell deaf kids to wear their hearing aids, especially when they are teenagers.

I missed out on so much in my late teens and early twenties. I felt like I was different but didn't really know why. My hearing loss was not talked about at my house. I was moody and always worried about my looks. I thought that my sister was more popular than me and prettier. During my teens I focused on keeping my long blonde hair washed and shiny and trying to look like Carol Lyndley, the popular movie star at the time. I also focused on boys. Somehow I suppose I did manage to get some studying done. At school I was not comfortable at lunch hour or in groups of girls because I couldn't follow the conversations that well. I guess I sought the attention from boys that I might have achieved with my girlfriends had I been able to hear better. I also know that I was very close to my mother and not close to my father. My mother always made things "right" for me and my father scared me to death. If I didn't answer right away at the table during dinner he would scream at me. My father also did not like me spending any time with boyfriends. I was glad that my father traveled so much so that my sister and I were mainly raised by my mother.

The beginning of my senior year in high school was 1961 after President Kennedy had been in office nine months. That August our family moved to Lausanne, Switzerland, where my father opened a branch office of his New York firm. My younger sister, Frances, and I were enrolled in a Swiss private school that followed an American College Board program. The classes were taught in French - a slow French, but French nonetheless. My former audiologist, James Healey, could never figure out how I learned French with a hearing loss but I guess I liked the language and conversing with others. I had studied a couple of years of French at Beard with Mlle. Angenot, which helped prepare me. The classes at the Ecole Nouvelle de la Suisse Romande were pretty small and the teacher attentive, with a good strong voice that I could hear. I managed to graduate from the school albeit not having any real science or American history courses. I did learn about Swiss history, however. My sister, a year younger than me, had more difficulty with French and my parents sent her to another Swiss private school for a year before she was able to graduate to attend an American college.

When it was time to go to college my mother said, "Look, dear, there is a new American college opening in Paris." So off my mother and I went to Paris, only five hours away by train from Lausanne. We met other students and parents from around the world at the college. My mom found a friendly, divorced French lady, Madame Renard, and her young son as a family for me to live with in the acceptable sixteenth *arron- dissement* or section of Paris. I loved Paris because the city was our campus and the cultural program that was included in our curriculum permitted us to attend all kinds of museums, operas, plays, art exhibits and historical places.

"Today you are going to visit the café on the Left Bank where James Joyce wrote ' Ulysses,' stated Professor Spicehandler, our English professor, on sabbatical from Columbia University, "and your next assignment will be to visit the Jeu de Paume" (the Impressionist museum at that time). I remember standing in front of Renoir's "The Lady on the Swing" and contemplating it at length before going home and writing the assigned theme that earned me an "A" in Spicehandler's class. I loved going to the art exhibits in Paris. It was probably easier to focus on the visual than on the audio for me.

The students in my class were to be the first graduating class from the American College in Paris. That celebration would take place in 1964, two years after we arrived in the city. Those two years in Paris were memorable ones for me. It was during the socially conscious early sixties when civil rights groups were marching for freedom in Washington and Vietnamese students in Paris were rioting on the Left Bank before the onset of the Vietnamese conflict. At the college we heard from notable political speakers such as Pierre Salinger, Kennedy's press secretary, and Richard Nixon, later to be president. Then there was the day late in November 1963. My roommate, Loretta James, and I had just climbed the four flights of stairs to our apartment to find the nasty little landlady, "Madame" as we called her, waiting behind the door as we entered. This time she wasn't waiting to chastise us for dating unsuitable *garçons* or leaving pots in the sink. She had been listening to her radio and she was crying. She shared with us the news of Kennedy's assassination. It seemed that all of Paris was weeping as we went out to walk on the Champs Elysees at eleven o'clock that night. There a continual parade of marchers kept a silent vigil up and down the wide boulevard, where two decades before the Americans had liberated France from the Germans.

For two years I explored the "City of Light" with friends, sometimes at all hours of the night. I strolled Les Halles by the hanging beef carcasses, ate onion soup after a night at the theater and composed poetry on the islands in the Seine. I also played silly student pranks with Loretta, such as pouring water from our apartment window over the heads of the moviegoers who had just left the cinema below us. Sometimes I would find original poetry left for me under the door in the morning from a boyfriend at the college named Charles. And sometimes that same boyfriend would leave me the most perfect of flowers that he had found at the nearby *marché*. I was also attending concerts with several Frenchmen whom I had met on the *France* crossing the Atlantic or at the international student dining hall in Paris. I did not lack for amusements, such as going for rides in the country, visiting Mont St. Michel and the castles of the Loire. Once I appeared on the cover of the American College in Paris catalog in front of Chateau Chenonceau holding hands with a young man that I would hear from forty years later, though I would not remember his name or who he was. My social life was great and existed primarily on a one-on-one basis where I could hear better.

In class at the college I was struggling to pass my courses without a hearing aid. My head swiveled like an owl's in order to try to read all the lips of the students in our class discussions. I loved learning about Plato and Aristotle in philosophy and even wrote poetry related to it that was published in the European Herald Tribune. I desperately wanted to be a part of the student discussions as I had so much to contribute in philosophy and psychology classes but I couldn't hear well enough to keep up with the topic. In some courses such as economics, whose professor was impossible for me to hear and whose topic was foreign, I just took a poor grade. After two years in Paris and a beautiful graduation with Sargent Shriver (later to be American ambassador to France and founding director of the Peace Corps) as the speaker and the choir singing "*Çe Mois de Mai*" it was time to leave and continue my education in the States. I was armed with a nearly perfect 800 score on my French college boards, primarily from learning idiomatic expressions and mingling with the people of France and Switzerland (which says something about how living in a foreign country helps to get the high board scores in that language) and many fond memories.

My mother had chosen the college for me to transfer in the States. It was Mary Washington College in Fredericksburg, Virginia, which had an audiology major. This college for women was deemed most appropriate for me by my mother and father. My mother felt that being an audiologist would be a well-suited vocation for me with a hearing loss. I wasn't sure. Being some- what emotionally immature and dependent on my mother, I wasn't sure what I wanted at that time. I did think that I wanted to remain in Europe. However, my father, who was European born, was set on sending my sister and me back to the USA for our education, where he believed there were more opportunities for young people. My father also liked the idea that Mary Washington was an all-female college. I think my father was afraid of my going away and being near young men. My mother used to make most of the decisions for me. I believe that she even wrote most of my college entrance autobiogra- phies. I didn't realize that until many years later, after her death, when I found some papers that she had kept about my college. She was protective, as are many parents of children with disabilities, and although she really thought that she was helping me, it may have been enabling. I believe, however, that she meant well, as I know she loved me very much.

Instead of being driven to the dorm by my parents, like most students, with a car full of bedding and books, I was driven to the French House at Mary Washington by my elderly god-mother, Naomi Hicklin from Princeton, New Jersey. Naomi was originally Welsh with a British accent and had danced with the famous Russian dancer, Pavlova's troupe when it came to the United States. (I used to play dress up with her old ballet tutus in the attic in Maplewood when I was growing up.) Naomi loved me like a daughter as she had no children of her own. I had said "Goodbye" to my parents at the airport in Geneva. I took off on the BOAC plane by myself, in spite of my father's pessi-mistic parting comments ("Look, she's going up the wrong ramp - what a screwball she is!") and arrived at New York safely where Naomi picked me up. Then we had set off for Mary Washington in Virginia.

The French House was a small dorm where the girls were friendly and welcoming. They were excited to have someone who had lived in Paris and spoke French. This was also where I was christened with my new name. The president of the French dormitory who greeted me, called me "Marie" instead of my complete name of Marie Maude, (which I didn't like anyway while growing up and I always made my sister and friends call me "Mary" instead. This is why my sister still calls me Mary). Marie has stuck even though I have added several surnames to that sobriquet in my lifetime.

Classes at MWC were tough. I was still not wearing any hearing aids. Biology was in a huge auditorium where I could not hear or understand a thing. I had no idea what The Krebs's

Cycle was (it hadn't helped that I had studied no science to speak of in the Swiss lycee except for a few weeks of studying "*Les Vers*" in the regular curriculum of French speaking classes at Ecole Nouvelle, but that got me into college). I relied entirely on textbooks or nice students who would share their notes. I absolutely hated the audiology professor, who had a tiny little voice and droned on ineffectively. I could hardly hear him. The excellent professors at The American College in Paris had spoiled me and I missed that quality of teaching. I was also an emotionally immature, homesick student who missed her family in Switzerland.

This set the perfect scene for a tall, dark and handsome young Marine officer from nearby Quantico Officers Training School to enter my life. I met Lt. Burrows T. Younkin, Jr. or "Jay" on a blind date, and before we knew it we were in love. Jay made me feel special and wanted to act as my knight in shining armor to take over and manage my life. I interpreted this as true love and followed everything he said. I did not have much confidence in myself and I was lonely and flattered that this handsome marine was taken by me. When Jay found out that I had a hearing loss, he said that was great because he needed someone who needed him. But my folks were furious, especially my father, who had invested much in my college education for my future. He sent my mother over to stop the whole thing but it didn't work. Jay and I got married in a small wedding at an Episcopal church in Fredericksburg in March and that was the end of my short stint at Mary Washington College. My parents did not come to the wedding and my aunt came down from New York to help me organize it. I thought that it would certainly be easier to be married than to struggle to hear the classes at MWC. Little did I know.

2

I Had My Activation Today

June 5

E va turned it on. Nothing happened. Then she made it louder. "Oww!" What a squeaky, awful noise I heard. My face screwed up. Kayla, my thirteen year old granddaughter, who had been so excited, now revealed disappointment on her face. I tried to talk and my words came out haltingly and slowly as if I had to think of each one because my voice was killing my ears. I told my family in a whispery tone that I could not stand my voice so they would not have to worry about me talking so much anymore. Myron, my husband and Dawne and Kayla started laughing. But Eva Bero, the warm and gentle audiologist at UMass Memorial in Worcester, kept talking to me with her calm and even tempered voice as I valiantly tried to adjust to these Mickey Mouse, hollow and resonant sounding, clicky noises coming out of my mouth. Meanwhile, Myron was recording all this on the camcorder for future reference. After a few minutes the sounds were more manageable and not so painful. Eva, with her professional manner, continued to talk while she adjusted my processor by programming on her computer as she had been doing for an hour or so. Her soft voice was starting to seem more familiar to me. "Now I will explain about the accessories that go with your processor in the kit". Then she demonstrated the collection of technical items provided. After a while I started to fade out as it was getting too hard to focus on the changing sounds in my head as well as the various advanced technology she was demonstrating. Even though I was tired I realized that Eva had a plan with her continuous talking. I felt like I was being forced to listen so that my brain could be given this opportunity to get accustomed to a new way of hearing.

By the time we left Eva's office I was feeling a little more calm and comfortable. I walked outside into the city streets. The noises from the cars did not seem offensive. We went to a cafe and the background noises were manageable and not painful. As Myron and I were driving home and I was talking to him about the experience I realized that my voice was starting to sound more "normal" and I was not whispering anymore. "Your voice sounds better", said Myron. We put the radio on and I heard the words, "sunny and warm," as I started to decipher some of the weather forecast and other words on talk radio. (I had never been able to understand talk radio before this). Then Myron's voice came out of a fog.

"What time do we have to be in East Greenwich"? I could actually hear him when I wasn't facing him! We changed the channel on the radio to find a music station. I could hear the music after agonizing over whether I would ever hear music again! That was one of the main reasons I had delayed getting the implant. Things were definitely getting better.

On the way home we were to attend my son's daughter, Emily's pre-school graduation. The entire time that I stayed in that huge room full of people my head was killing me. It felt like I was hearing a ragtime piano playing loudly and off tune in my ear—definitely nerve wracking.

"This is your brain trying to find something it can relate to when it hasn't used those nerve endings in such a long time", said Myron.

"I guess my brain relates to off tune ragtime piano players but the rest of me doesn't," I replied.

When we went outside, away from the crowd, the excruciating noise started to go away and I started to feel better. What a relief!

When we arrived home I had to go to the bathroom right away. While I was on the toilet I heard a loud noise. So now I have a choice, I thought, to pee silently when not wearing my processor or to pee with this incredible rush of sound like a huge waterfall. Perhaps I will get used to it. Later that evening, I was about to rest but first wanted to share my experience with my family and friends through e-mail. I thanked my family and friends for their love and support along the way of this incredible journey. I had made a commitment and a lot of expensive equipment was now in my head so I knew I couldn't go back. I was determined to persevere with this and get better and better with hearing.

June 7

Today I went for my second mapping in Worcester with Eva. A little more about Eva Bero, as she has been such a big part of my progress with my implant: Eva is an audiologist who is able to combine her strong technical skills with positive communication and interpersonal relationships. She is open and non-threatening, in her early thirties, with no accent and she dresses simply to avoid distractions. As an undergraduate, she majored in Brain and Cognitive Sciences instead of Speech and Hearing in her Audiology program. She still has a strong interest in research regarding understanding the importance of human perception processing beyond the cochlea. She worked in Boston at Mass Eye and Ear before she came to UMass Worcester to develop the Cochlear Implant program and have a direct impact on implant team/decision making as the clinical coordinator. She worked with Dr. Lee and is the liaison with the operating room, administration, CI manufacturers, research, patient and professional groups to give the best patient care.

Eva tested me by speaking in a normal voice and covering her mouth so I couldn't lip read. (I am an excellent lip reader from years of experience). I understood 100% of the words she asked me on the first board. Then she decided to try a more difficult board that she does not ordinarily use with a client after only two days of activation. This time I only missed one word. Eva was smiling.

"You are really doing well."

My friend, Judy, who had accompanied me, started to cry.

In the afternoon I attended my granddaughters' Stella and Emily's ballet recitals. This time I was able to hear the music playing for the dances and I could even understand some of the lyrics of the songs the children sang. There was not as much "ringing" accompaniment so it was much more comfortable. My brain was getting used to the sounds of music. In the car I was listening to a talk show on the National Public Radio station. It felt strange to enjoy the jokes and information that was broadcast. I was never able to understand talk radio before or hear the punch lines.

June 14

Earlier this afternoon I was back at Eva's office and she gave me some more informal tests. This time I was to answer simple conversational questions or complete sentences while Eva's mouth was covered. All my answers were correct.

"I am going to give you another round of sentences that are not related to each other in content".

I recognized all of them except that I said "blue" in one sentence instead of "green" or the other way around. Words not related in content are more difficult to recognize. Anyway, Eva was thrilled.

"You are doing so well for only one week after activation and for someone who has had such a bad hearing loss for such a very long time. You have now progressed as far as where others might be at several months down the line".

We will see what happens when I go back in a few weeks for more formalized testing in the booth.

3

Joy In My Heart

June 13

This is an exciting new life. I have been trying all kinds of things to see how I can hear. Tonight I tried my first phone calls with my implant ear on our Captel phone. I called my daughter, Joy, and I could hear and understand her voice, although it did sound unfamiliar to me. Then I called Dawne and heard her voice but it was a little strange also. These differences will work out with time. I called Sharon, my eldest, and distinctly understood the messages left on her answering machine. Oh, glory! It has been such a long time since I have been able to understand anything on the phone and I have felt so isolated. Right now I am not even supposed to be ready to use the phone yet. I am so elated. I have to be careful that I don't get too excited, actually, as it feels frightening to feel so happy.

I thought I would try to see if I could sing. I grabbed the Broadway songbook and started in. First it was "All I Ask of You" from *Phantom of the Opera* and I really think I hit those high notes. Then I tried "Memory", one of my favorite songs, as I walked around the kitchen singing to myself and evaluating my success. Then I went on to "Climb Ev'ry Mountain", a song I have always loved. I ran into the other room and tried all the piano keys to see which ones I could hear. Before the implant I could not hear any of the high notes above the middle octave range. Now I can hear every single one of the high frequency notes! Oh what ecstasy! Maybe my dreams of singing on Broadway are not over after all at the age of sixty-three. What new mountains will there be to climb in my life? Watch out everyone, I will at least be able to make another debut at the True Brew Cafe, a local place where I had celebrated my sixtieth birthday by singing, (probably off key) dancing and being the emcee.

Another strange thing is happening since the implant activation. I find myself waking up more easily each morning with more joy in my heart. Eva says it is because I had such a profound loss before that it took so much energy just to make my way through the day trying to communicate with everyone or straining to listen. I was probably weary and sometimes even depressed so it was hard to get going in the morning. Now I am excited to get up and I look forward to seeing what the day is going to bring and what I will hear. What new information will I learn from the radio or from other people that will make my world more fascinating? There is new vitality inside me and I can feel it. I think it is evident as I am getting positive comments from others about how young I look.

Sometimes I think about my mother at this juncture in my hearing progress. My mother, Martha Richey Neubert, was born in Cincinnati, Ohio, in 1908. Her father, The Reverend Francis Richey, was an Episcopal clergyman whose mother, Emma Cecelia Bacot, my great grandmother, was from a French Huguenot family in Charleston, South Carolina, who had left the South after the Civil War and come up North to marry an Irishman. My mother's mother, Mary Elizabeth Lowe, was from Virginia from an old English family. My mother was an only child whose childhood included trips abroad with her aunt and uncle, Maud and Samuel Seabury, who had no children of their own. Judge Samuel Seabury fought Mayor Walker and the corruption at Tammany Hall in New York in the early nineteen thirties. Mother went to Smith College and met my father, Adolph Neubert, from Austria while she was spending her junior year studying in France. Had my mother been a woman in today's generation she most certainly would have been a lawyer or perhaps even a politician. After my father died, my mother did get involved in politics on eastern Long Island and was the acting village mayor of North Haven. She lived for more than twenty years as a very independent widow on Long Island who lead a rich and full life participating in many civic and cultural activities to enhance the community. Her memorial service in Sag Harbor was attended by hundreds of people who had many stories to tell about her accomplishments. I was close to my mother, proud of her and somewhat in awe of her.

When I was a little girl Mother spent many days taking me to audiologists around the country. I have a memory of taking the same tests over and over again. "Say the word baseball". "Say the word hot dog". I think I probably memorized them all. When my mom found out that I had a hearing loss as a young child, she was devastated and did everything in her power to help me. There was no Americans with Disabilities Act then to assist students. My mom read everything she could, contacted experts, prepared the way with my teachers and finally put me in a private school with small classes. She reminded me to lower my voice and to enunciate and she corrected my mispronunciations. As a teen she let me take private dramatic arts lessons so I could learn more about speech and drama. She constantly believed in me and encouraged me in all my endeavors. How I wish my mom could see me now! She would be so happy to know that I am going to have "nearly normal" experiences with communication, at the age of sixty-three. I must think that she does know and I expect that she is up there now looking down at me and marveling at this miracle that is allowing me to hear so much better. God bless my Mom.

4

Planes Without Ringing And Other Discoveries

June 14

Sometimes I forget I can hear. I was walking around in the living room and I heard a man on the radio in a commercial talking about how great Mitsubishi cars are. I am so used to hearing muffled sounds as "voices" on the radio that I found myself stopping and wondering where "that voice" was coming from. Oh, and I can't wait to hear the voice of "that other man" in our bedroom where Myron installed the emergency radio system that tells what storms are headed our way. It has just been unintelligible garbled noises so I wondered why it was in our bedroom in the first place but I guess Myron can understand it. I will have to wait for a storm or a hurricane to practice listening to that voice.

It also feels odd to be in line at the cashier and actually catch what people around me are saying. I used to keep my head looking down because I couldn't hear what was said around me and I didn't want to be embarrassed by misunderstanding. I even asked a friend once, "What do people talk about when they are standing in line or sitting at the next booth in a restaurant?" I was curious to know, as a writer, because someday I would be working on a novel and I would need to master dialogue. Yesterday I was in line at Job Lot and the cashier made a joke as she handed me my two pennies change.

"Well, I have to get my two cents worth in," she said, as I marveled at my ability to understand what she was saying. I wondered how many of those friendly comments I might have missed while standing across from cashiers, facing down, afraid to miss something directed to me or God forbid, answering a question the wrong way. I used to prepare myself before I went to the super market by deciding ahead of time whether I wanted paper or plastic so I could be quick on the draw when the cashier gave me that quizzical look and I could tell her which bags I wanted." Paper, oh no, plastic, it's raining out!" Now I try to remember to take my own recyclable bags too.

Perhaps with my new implant I will start to like cafeterias, counters and cash registers. I will feel more confident when I hear the Dunkin' Donuts clerk ask me, "cream or sugar?" I heard her this morning and managed to get my order correct with minimal confusion at the donut shop. Hoorah! Then I heard "Good morning, Marie," and there was my "morning coffee" pal, Ann, sitting over in the corner of the shop, surrounded by background noise and I did not have to read her lips! At this point in my progress background noise that my brain has not recognized or become familiar with is registering as a low ringing sound in my processor. The medical professionals tell me that in a few months the ringing will go away as the nerve endings in my brain start to get more familiar with the different sounds and they will be able to handle the increased sound input. How exciting.

Speaking of ringing, this morning I was out in my garden and there was a terrible ringing going on. I looked all around trying to identify the sound. Finally I looked up and saw a plane flying overhead. It's like that now but it will get better. Planes without ringing are in my future. I must be patient. I can't recognize cars yet while on my walk but I do hear a ringing when the cars are coming near. This is when Myron or a friend pulls me over to the side of the road, thank goodness. In time I will be able to recognize the real sounds that cars make and not have ringing.

In preparation for my surgery I had placed the chaise lounge in the middle of the living room facing the television with a small table laden with books, drinks and snacks next to it. At first it may have been a little difficult for Myron to watch me reclining like Queen Mary on the chaise while he was doing his usual work and increased household duties. Myron was wondering why I was not able to empty the dishwasher or fold the laundry during the first week of my recuperation. We needed to have a little talk and then Myron realized how important it was for me to rest and relax. That was when we decided to engage the assistance of the lovely Caring Connection ladies of our church who brought meals over for us for about a week. This was helpful and took the pressure off the stress of the early evenings when Myron and I would not have to worry about what was for supper. I have to say that Myron has been an incredible help with this whole process and it *is* a process and a large commitment. While you are recuperating you need the assistance of someone to help you with meals and household chores. Myron has his own business at home so fortunately he was nearby. If you are thinking of a cochlear implant it is so helpful to have a supportive spouse or close friends to be there for you as in any kind of surgery recovery. I was fortunate to have both and they made my journey to healing so much easier.

It was very hard for me to not be busy the first week as I realized that I am probably a type "A" person in spite of my preaching otherwise. But by the second week I had really started to enjoy relaxing and taking it easy in the slower lane of life. I have since incorporated the concept of balance into my schedule more and I find that I listen to my body and rest when I am tired. I don't think of life as a continual run on a treadmill. This really serves no purpose except to provide exhaustion. Perhaps many could benefit from this pattern in life which would be healthier all around.

My resting chaise position in the center of our living room gave me an opportunity to practice what I preach on my cable television show. *"Tea with Marie"* is my Rhode Island show that focuses on positive aspects of life related to beauty, gentility and tranquility. I serve my guests tea and we discuss topics connected to beauty such as art, music, literature or other areas. While resting I found that I became more in tune with the changes of the light during the day, an enjoyment of the subtle shades of transparent beauty. My chaise was facing the lilacs blooming outside as well as the flowers in my sunroom. At times I found myself feeling more calm and relaxed in my body and truly appreciating some of the simple joys in life. I was focusing more on aspects of beauty and basic things that I had not always noticed around me.

I sit here writing on my computer in a cozy corner of my sun room confronted by the large salmon pink geranium plants in the opposite corner. Just outside the surrounding windows my garden is beginning to become inundated with small red and light pink roses. I find that I can actually hear the soft classical music of Mozart on the radio that is located just inside the other room. And there is no ringing accompaniment! And to think that I could not hear *anything* that was in another room before this. Life continues on with its many miracles of sound.

5

More New Discoveries And Thoughts

June 15

This morning I sat on a bench on my deck and wept, feeling overwhelmed by new experiences. The bright blue sky with cumulus clouds floated above and the birds flitted from bush to tree around my garden. Cardinals, wrens, finches and sparrows were darting across the yard, perching on trees and squabbling among themselves at the feeder. Hearing the birds is such a new experience for me. I think I am starting to distinguish among the various voices. There are the shrill shriekers, the sounds like whistling and the repetitious calling sounds. I can't tell which voice belongs to which bird yet. I find myself walking around the garden and talking to some of the birds. After hearing a long "tweet, tweet, tweet," I respond with a similar, "tweet, tweet, tweet, tweet" and we carry on a bird–to–human conversation going back and forth. I feel a new connection. This goes on for awhile until I am afraid the neighbors will wonder what I am doing.

Now I can call across the street to my neighbors and say more than a "Hi" and then walk away. I can say something like "Hi, Are you going to the beach today?" and then wait to hear the answer and get "No, not today, it is too cold." I am by nature a very outgoing person and I love to be friendly and enjoy the other people on this earth. This is part of why I think life is so special - to share and connect with each other. I have always been outgoing to a limited extent and I am beginning to see what a limited extent it has been. Now I can actually engage in a *conversation* when someone is farther than a foot away from me. I can talk to the neighbors and hear what they say back to me. It has been limiting for me over the years to create relationships with the neighbors when I could only call out a greeting and not be able to hear the answer. Sometimes I have been labeled as a snob by neighbors because I was not able to respond to them. This happened at Camp LeJeune at our officers housing complex. Yesterday I discovered that many of our neighbors actually say "Hi, Marie" when they pass by. Now I can say, "Hi, Richard" or "Hi, Joyce" or "Hi, Cricket" and not miss a beat. I think it will be fun to get to know the neighbors better by talking with them.

For the past year or so I have noticed that whenever I pass a bus on the road that is coming toward me, the same thing happens. It is a small thing. But sometimes even small things can carry messages for us if we want. The bus sign, at the top of the bus, changes *just* at the moment when I am facing the bus from my car. Maybe this happens to everyone, I don't know, but I decided that it had to have some meaning for me. I decided it meant a change was in store for me since I was witnessing these changes in destination signs on the buses every time I saw one. (It even happened to me on some recent trips to Washington and Chicago.) Now I know. My whole life is changing for the better and there are probably many more changes in store. It will be an unraveling tale of adventure for sure.

I have not yet allowed myself to become overly emotional about opening this new door to the world of hearing but I know it will happen soon when I am least expecting it. I have been so busy with my usual activities, the show, writing, garden, grandchildren, friends, committees and so on that I really didn't have time to think or feel anxious about the surgery until the pre-surgery visit a week before the actual surgery. This was good because I did not have the jitters for too long. Also, I went into this whole process with relatively few expectations, as one does not always know what the outcome will be. Perhaps that is part of why I am now having so much fun every day as I discover so many new aspects of life. How can I put it? It is as though everything else has taken a back seat in priorities in my life right now as I am focused on making discoveries and learning new things about the hearing world. I wonder if this is how babies feel when they first learn to hear and recognize words.

6

Thoughts From Sagabon

November 2008

From the time I was a small girl I remember going to Sagabon or "the country," as my mother called it, every summer. Mother packed up the car, the dog, my sister and myself and drove in to Manhattan from New Jersey to pick up my father at work. My father drove us down the island for a few hours until we reached Fresh Pond Road. It was always a contest to see who the first person in the family would be to shout out "I see Sagabon" as we rounded the pond that faced the old house, sitting at the top of the hill, at the end of the long driveway. The excitement that arose inside of me as a kid is the way I have always felt about Sagabon.

The mystique of Sagabon is hard to describe but I imagine that most of us have Sagabons in our minds. My memories of Sagabon are of a simple shingled farmhouse tucked in the corner of nature bordered by woods, ponds and fields of hay approached by long, sandy driveways flanked with several varieties of sweet and spicy smelling wild roses and honey suckle. There was also fragrant mint hidden in the corners of flower beds near the lavender and rosemary and strong wafts of boxwood hit your nose when you walked out the front door. The old photos show my grandmother, a stately woman with long auburn hair piled in a chignon, wearing a dress with beads around her neck as she stood smiling in the rose garden, sometimes with the aunts and sometimes with my grandfather. The mimosa trees were plentiful then and scattered about with their silky pink blossoms that I used to love to brush under anyone's neck I could catch to tickle them and giggle.

At Sagabon my sister and I learned about life and how to behave. Until our early teen years when our grandparents were alive, we had the influence of the Victorian and Edwardian era on a daily basis. My grandmother, Dearie, raised in Virginia, only entered the kitchen to make mayonnaise or to supervise the annual beach plum, grape jelly or pickled watermelon rind rituals. At those times she would sit on a stool, like a queen, and direct my mother, Margaret (her Irish maid) and anyone else who was lucky enough to have access to her orders. After my mother became the matriarch of Sagabon, she also, would direct anyone, staff or guests alike, to assist around the place and the funny thing was everyone loved being a part of things. I sometimes think that my sister and I have inherited that tendency and I hope our friends and family think it is fun.

It was indeed a matriarchal society in which I was raised. My grandmother held court at the dining room table by keeping the conversation flowing and my grandfather, the minister, and a man of few words, sat at the other end of the table next to me. Even my father, of strong mind and spirit, would defer to my grandmother. I never saw him argue with her. She had a gentle air and expected you to act that way also. She inspected the fingernails of my sister and myself from time to time to see if they were clean and expressed her dismay over the current slang in our English language such as the words "cute" or "cunning" which she did not like. Her daily afternoon teas were special occasions. I enjoyed watching everyone gather around Dearie, including the dog and any guests or nearby aunts, in the drawing room or screened porch. Then we waited for Margaret to bring the tea tray and wondered if there would be another treat besides the thin bread and butter, perhaps some Scottish shortbread or Danish coffee cake? It was a tea ceremony when my grandmother poured and there was a language that accompanied it. "One lump or two?" "Would you care for milk or lemon?" "Would you like some more hot water?" These memories were at the heart of my television show, *Tea with Marie*," and still remain with me as I take tea, either alone, with Myron or with my grandchildren or family and friends.

While we lived in Europe our dear friends, the Piersons, who grew to love Sagabon as their own, took care of the place for my parents. As a child, upstairs in my bed, I would spend hours at night listening to Hubert and Sally Pierson and other friends of my parents laughing together on the screened porch on balmy summer evenings. Many friends came to Sagabon from all over the world and left special comments about their visits. My sister and her husband, Doug, lived there with my mother for a while. Doug and Frani were married there. My mother arranged the wedding as my father had died a few years before. There was a large tent in front of the house, a band and dancing was held on the centuries-old wide floorboards in the dining room. The caterers were flitting back and forth from the kitchen to the tent. All summer my mother had nurtured the white impatiens around the property to be ready for the September wedding. My daughter, Sharon, was ten and a flower girl and Mother made the lemon-flavored wedding cake which I decorated and crowned with the Temple of Love that had sat on my mother and father's cake in 1934.

After my father died when my mother lived alone year round at Sagabon, she created an enriched world for herself. She entertained writers and artistic friends at dinner parties, became involved in local politics, was acting deputy mayor, served on the church vestry and was busy with the Friends of the Library. When we went to visit while my children were small Mother would make life so pleasant for us, as I have mentioned before. My mother taught my children about some of the gracious elements of life by helping them learn manners and by being an example, as a lover of nature, the arts and culture. My children looked forward to our visits to Sagabon (especially during our family's rough years) and still speak of it as a sanctuary. I also found it to be a refuge of tranquility and replenishment where you could go to recharge your batteries.

The nature, the continuity of family and the generosity and love coming from my mother was nurturing for all of us.

A few years after my mother died, my sister and I realized that we could no longer keep Sagabon. It was the end of an era. Four generations had enjoyed life in the home that had once been a seventeenth-century farm house near a salt mine. Over the years Sagabon had expanded to accommodate the needs of the families that lived and loved inside its walls. Perhaps that was the mystique of Sagabon. It was a "spirit of place" as D.H. Lawrence wrote, and a spirit that will live on in the dreams of all those who have ever lived or visited there.

7

The Marriage To Jay

1965

After we were married Jay and I moved to Camp Lejeune, North Carolina, where he was stationed as a second lieutenant in the US Marine Corps. We rented a tiny apartment outside the base where I knew no one but there was a swimming pool outside which was nice in that hot weather. The apartment complex looked like a long modern motel. I felt lonely and depended entirely on Jay's company when he came home from work. It was hard to be away from familiar friends and places. Then we moved into base housing, which was more comfortable. The lieutenants' quarters were ranch houses so we had more room and close neighbors. I found a small abandoned puppy on our doorstep that we adopted and called "Mini". I couldn't hear a lot of the neighbors who came outside and probably said "Hi" but I did get to know a nice lady next door. In the humid southern afternoons I went to her air-conditioned house to watch soap operas and drink Coca-Colas. My family was still in Switzerland.

One day in October Jay came home unexpectedly at lunch-time and told me to sit down. By that time I was pregnant and happily decorating the nursery.

Jay said, "I have orders."

"What does that mean?" I asked.

"It means that I have orders for Camp Pendleton, which is in California on the way to Vietnam. Now don't worry, just get a suitcase together and I will be back to pick you up this after-noon and drive you to Rhode Island to be with my folks. Then I will come back and close up everything here."

Shocked isn't the word for how I felt. It was more like un-real. He had orders on the day our first baby was due to be born.

I'll never forget the ride from Camp Lejeune to Rhode Island, a trip of about eighteen hours. I lay in a bed that Jay had concocted for me in the back seat of the old fifties pale blue Plymouth "shark" with the big fins. Mini rode shotgun in the front seat with Jay. Every five minutes or so Jay would turn around and ask if I had any pains. We managed to finally arrive in Woonsocket, Rhode Island, where Jay's parents (whom I hardly knew) lived. Jay's parents were the complete opposite of my parents. They were two large, overweight adults whose idea of fun was loading into the car after an early sup-per and driving to the nearby Dairy Queen for dessert. My mother-in-law,

Peggy, worked as a nurses aide and my father-in-law, Bert, was a supervisor at the US Rubber plant nearby. My mother-in-law, in particular, surprised me with her coarse language and her continuous bragging about her son and herself. I can't repeat some of the things she used to say.

Jay left me with his parents in their small three bedroom ranch house and turned around a few hours later to return to North Carolina and close up our base housing. After that he drove right back to Woonsocket. At the moment when he walked into the house looking tired and gray, my water broke and he had to take me to the hospital. Fortunately for him (but not me) my labor was fourteen hours long so he could go home and get some rest. I had the baby (Sharon Rose) at 1 A.M. on Halloween. She was quickly dubbed "Punkin Younkin" by the nurses. That weekend my parents came back from Switzer-land, and it was the first time my father and Jay would meet each other. I was glad to be in the hospital by myself when that meeting took place. Two weeks later, against the doctor's orders, I took off with Jay driving across the country for Camp Pendleton: A twenty-one-year-old new mother and a twenty-three-year-old father. My mother-in-law said it was the bravest thing I ever did. I think it was the only nice thing she ever said about me. As I look back I realize it was nuts.

We were only at Camp Pendleton for a few weeks when Jay put me on a plane to return to Rhode Island and he took off later that night on another plane for Vietnam. I was carrying the baby dressed in her hand-knit pink sweater set and I was crying copious tears. The pilot, who was walking out to the plane, carried the diaper bag for me as I guess he thought I was in bad shape. The dog was in a carrying crate, where she would remain for more than twelve hours. I couldn't eat anything on the plane. My stomach felt like saw dust. When we arrived near Providence there was a major blizzard so the plane had to fly to Boston to land. From Boston to Providence I had to ride in a limo with some businessmen because the airline wouldn't let me on the transport bus with the dog. The businessmen were very kind and so was the chauffeur. The driver immediately let me walk the dog while the businessmen waited. One of the businessmen was holding the baby. My in-laws picked me up at the airport in Providence.

Jay was in Vietnam for fifteen months. During that time my parents moved back to the US. I stayed with them during the summer in Sag Harbor, at "Sagabon". My father started to come around and was getting more used to having an extended family. I used to catch him speaking baby talk to Sharon while she was in her playpen. That September I gave birth to our second child, Burrows Thomas, III, at Southampton Hospital. My father went around telling everyone, "We finally have a boy!"

Two weeks before Tommy was born I had suddenly stopped getting the letters from Jay that I had been receiving every day. I had vicious nightmares and stomachaches. Then during my labor at the hospital my mother brought me a letter from Jay. I was so relieved but my son was born with a peptic ulcer probably related to my stomachaches. It took five months for a doctor to finally diagnose and control this problem. Tommy got rid of the ulcer and was much better. The two children were ten and a half months apart so I nursed Tommy while my Mom took care of Sharon.

When Jay returned from Vietnam we moved back to Rhode Island after another stint at Camp Lejeune. I spent the "year from hell" at Jay's mother's house in Woonsocket while he got his masters degree at Rhode Island College. Jay's father had died before we left Camp Lejeune and the agreement between Jay's mother and himself was that she would go to nursing school, Jay to get his masters and I would tend the house including our two little ones, Jay's retarded sister, Sherry, our dog, Mini and my mother-in-law's undisciplined Weimeraner. I was never consulted about the arrangement. I think I was regarded as a child because I couldn't hear everything. I was hoping that Jay would accept one of the lucrative offers from Conoco or a few other companies that were pursuing him as a retiring decorated USMC captain. Instead, I found myself being accosted at the end of a hair raising day by Peggy about the rug being too dirty or the chicken not being cooked well enough. I had no car, money or friends available to me, just continuous work without relief except for teaching Sunday school on Sunday mornings. Jay would head off to college early in the morning and return about midnight. That Thanksgiving at my parents' condo in New Jersey, with tears in my eyes, I begged to stay there, but my mother said "Be a Puritan and stay by your husband where you belong". I often wonder why I didn't leave then but I had no career, no way to hear and I would never have had my next two children who are beloved by me. Apparently, no self esteem either.

When we moved to Narragansett where Jay began a PhD program in biochemistry at the University of Rhode Island I was ecstatic: A home of our own again, away from Peggy and her despotic demands. We had two more children, Dawne Marie and Joy Margaret, four children in six years. Jay would get up in the middle of the night as I couldn't hear the children call. He usually talked to the kids more as I would not always hear what was going on and this gave him a definite advantage in developing relationships with them. However, I was very involved as a mother, in spite of my hearing loss and creatively presided over the children's activities. Jay's graduate studies lasted for nearly eight years and it was a period of many struggles and stresses with economics and emotions. There were ups and downs. Perhaps Jay's stay in Viet Nam influenced his inability to concentrate better on the job at hand and to avoid temptations along the way. There were times when we ran out of money and we would have to raid the piggy bank to buy milk for the baby. It was the time before credit cards so we didn't buy anything if we didn't have the money. Jay started to work nights at Rhode Island Hospital and go to school during the day. When we were broke Jay used to tell me to "have faith" and when a check from my parents would arrive in the mailbox he would say, "See, I told you to have faith!" One Christmas my parents gave us new tires for the car because we could barely drive on the ones we had.

Jay was at the university most of the time or working in the lab or the hospital. I was lonely and getting tired of having no money. In spite of our indigence, however, I enjoyed many good times with our children. It was an imaginative household. Halloween found Sharon's birthday combined with a haunted house set up in the basement. There were driveway talent shows for the summertime fund when we induced the neighbors take part as the audience. When I couldn't go back to Austria on the tenth anniversary of my dancing with Hohenzollerns and Hapsburgs in the Schloss Schonbrunn in Vienna, I designed Heuriger parties in our basement that was decorated with grapevines and "old country" linen table-clothed card tables. The little girls performed ballet opening dances that I had choreographed and then they waited on tables with their waitress outfits made by Mom. The neighbors were always waiting to see what the next unusual event was going to be. We had no money but we had a lot of creativity.

Then there was always Sagabon in the summer time. Sagabon became our refuge, especially with my mother there to make everything so perfect for our visits.

One day at the beach near Sagabon, about eight years after I was married, a friend of ours, Mike Lennon, also in a PhD program, said to me:

"Marie, why the hell don't you wear your hearing aid?"

This was one of the turning points of my life. I located my old hearing aid in a bureau drawer. Of course it was broken. I took it to the Rhode Island Office of Rehabilitation Services in

Providence where they paid to have my hearing aid repaired and eventually bought me a new one. ORS also introduced me to their many other services. I could receive glasses to assist in reading lips and George Bond, a rehabilitation counselor, said that I could return to school to prepare for a career and they would help me with this.

"Go back to school," I thought, "how wonderful."

I rushed out to register as a special student at the University of Rhode Island with my hearing aid planted firmly in my ear. No more feeling embarrassed or shy about the hearing aid. I was more mature. I knew that it would open doors for me. I started college again with an English literature course, as that was my most familiar area. Soon I had to face biology and I found that I actually enjoyed it. I liked it so much that I continued taking more advanced science courses such as biochemistry, quantitative cell culture and histology and I actually majored in biology. And this was the course that I could not hear or pass at Mary Washington College! I also took a minor in French and I graduated cum laude from URI in 1976 as an older student, ten years, four kids and one husband later than if I had graduated with my original college class in 1966. ORS claimed that I was one of their best advertisements and I realized that the right tools can make a big difference.

The four children were growing up, attending school, playing Little League and going to ballet. I was struggling with teaching science and straining to hear the students. Things were becoming difficult between Jay and myself. There was a lot of anger and arguing. Then my mother became ill with Lou Gehrig's disease. She had been with my sister in Pennsylvania but now she wanted to go back to Sagabon. So I went to Sagabon to take care of her. Jay was home coaching Joy and Dawne's Little League team and refusing to let the girls go to visit their dying grandmother. He did eventually let Tom and a friend go down to visit. I spent the summer trying to keep my mother as comfortable as possible and attempting to make some sense out of my life. My mother was dying and my marriage was falling apart. No wonder I had lost fifteen pounds that summer and looked skinny in a bikini. Friends of my mother were great and came around often and helped me. The Sisters of Mercy were a godsend as they instructed me every day about my mother's physical and emotional needs.

My mother was brave as she gradually lost her various physical abilities. She never complained and she was always a mother who cared about the welfare of her children. She even ordered food from a friend's cook so that I would have something to eat while caring for her. That was the kind of mother she was. I was still my mother's child with a hearing loss that was getting worse and no way of understanding what life was going to be like after she passed away and my marriage dissolved.

At the end of the summer my mother died in the same bedroom where her mother had died. All of her family was around her, including her grandchildren, taking turns during the last nightly vigil. In spite of the tragedy of the disease and the end of our cherished mother and grandmother, it was a natural and beautiful way for her to die, near her garden and at her beloved Sagabon. The very next day the children of our close friends and our family members were helping to pack the station wagon to take Sharon, our eldest, to her first year at Swarthmore College, while the adults were planning the memorial service for Mother.

After returning to Rhode Island, my marriage really fell apart and Jay left. My hearing ear dog, "Stubby" died and I became a single adult raising three teenage children. I was scared and I felt alone. For about a week I shivered and shook at night, not knowing what the unfamiliar sounds were that I heard without my hearing aids.

8

At Church

My sister and I grew up going to church nearly every Sunday with my mother and grandmother. I remember my grandmother, Dearie, singing the hymn, "Holy, Holy, Holy" with her quivering eighty-year-old voice as I looked up at her dressed in something long, flowing and purple in Christ Church, the summer church we attended in Sag Harbor, Long Island. Sometimes in church I would watch my grandmother, a tall, dignified lady, bent over in her prayers and weeping in her pew. I imagined that she wept about family and friends who had passed on. We were not big weepers in my family, being WASPS and Huguenot descendants. My grandmother would sometimes tell me about how happy she was that her sister was in heaven but that she missed her very much. My grandfather, the Reverend Francis H. Richey, was an Episcopal priest and his daughter, Martha, my mother, an only child, was quite active in the church. Mother was in the vestry and the altar guild and she ran the Christmas pageant or

"Mystery" every year at St. George's in Maplewood, New Jersey. My father would either be playing tennis on Sunday mornings or singing in the choir. After church and Sunday school my mother would serve us a delicious Sunday dinner in the middle of the day. I marvel at how she prepared the dinner as well as served the nutritious hot English breakfasts, such as kippered herring or kidney stew with hominy grits and eggs *before* we left for Sunday School and church. And to think that we are fortunate to have bagels and coffee from Dunkin Donuts before church today.   Sundays could be tough for me growing up. At dinners Father would lose patience when I did not hear and answer him right away and he would yell. I was very tense at dinner hours. Sometimes I would daydream to escape and because it was easier than straining to listen.

In church I took to drifting into a dream world during the sermon. This became an automatic reaction. The sermon would come and it would be the signal for me to relax and enter a reverie where I could think about teenage thoughts such as boys and clothes. When I became an adult I depended on reading lips in church, especially after the service had ended and everyone stood up as the organ blasted the recessional. This was when everyone wanted to wish you "Good morning" and talk to you. I would engage the "deaf" nod and smile. Then we would file into the even noisier parish hall with the poor acoustics for coffee hour and I would attempt to lip read with the background noise. More challenges for the hard of hearing. I would bob my head up and down as folks smiled and spoke to me. Who knows to what I was conceding? Coffee hour was becoming more and more frustrating.

About two years ago my husband and I changed churches and I let go of fifty years of loyalty to the Episcopal Church. At a local women's network meeting I had met a fascinating woman who was a Unitarian Universalist minister. After spending most of her life as a lawyer, Betty Kornitzer felt called to the ministry to find more spiritual fulfillment, help others and follow her conscience. She is a warm, caring and magnetic person who attracts many newcomers to her church. Myron, whose background is Jewish, and I took a trip to see what Betty's church was about and we both felt at home in the accepting community. The congregation transforms an American Legion bingo hall into a church sanctuary every Sunday morning. Parishioners drag chairs across the floor, close a dark curtain across the bingo board and prepare a simple altar as they set up before church. Then they put everything back in place after the service. The contrast of ornate stone churches with stained glass and organ music from my past with the simplicity of the bingo hall, forces me to focus on what I think matters most, which is the spirit of the place, the inspiring moments and the special people we find there. The minister uses a microphone which is helpful for Myron and me. Others in the church are aware and assist in making sure people can hear as well as possible. Betty has asked me to translate certain prayers into American Sign Language before the congregation. No one signed when I first started doing this a year or so ago. Now as I look out at the congregation I see a hundred or more adults and children signing back. It is an incredible connection, personally, and a broader awareness and acceptance of other cultures for the church members.

Today I went to St. Luke's Episcopal Church in East Greenwich with my eldest daughter, Sharon. She had asked me to go with her as she was in a roll-over car accident a few weeks ago and she is lucky to be alive. She still has a serious wound on her arm as well as possible emotional scars. Usually I attend our Unitarian Universalist Church but I wanted to be with my daughter and keep her company today.

I was curious to see how I was going to handle the various aspects related to hearing that I would encounter at this church service after my implant. St. Luke's is a massive pseudo Gothic stone church that can seat five or six hundred parishioners. It was half full and the accompanying high ceilings and echoes were already proving a challenge. My first test was the hymns. I am familiar with the Episcopal hymns. At least I thought I was familiar with the hymns. Silently I was praising the Lord that I could hear music but I didn't know that the music would sound so strange! It seemed that the melodies were off and the pace was slower and more monotone. It was hard to follow the hymns, especially "The Naval Hymn," one of my favorites. So I cheated and read my daughter's lips to keep up with the tune. After the service, Sharon paid me the supreme compliment. "Ma, that was the first time I have ever heard you sing on tune in my entire life!" Wow. Just more encouragement for me to take singing lessons later on with Tina.

(Tina Bernard is a singing teacher at the University of Rhode Island, where I had taken a few voice lessons before my sixtieth birthday party shindig.)

The last time I was at St. Luke's I had struggled to hear the minister's sermon even though he uses a microphone. Eventually I "tuned out" and started to daydream, my usual habit. I did think about God, though, and counted my blessings. Well, this time with a little bit of effort and studious concentration I was able to understand most of the sermon. It was a challenge as I am not used to paying attention or listening and I had to work hard to focus. Being able to hear did not automatically mean that I could listen after not doing so for most of my life. I was also able to understand more from the lay readers and I did not have to concentrate so fully on the written words in the program in order to follow them.

Ah, and then there was the choir! St. Luke's has a wonderful choir. I did not know if I was ever going to hear music again in my life when I embarked on this implant project. I had refused a cochlear implant four years ago at Massachusetts Eye and Ear in Boston because I did not want to give up hearing music the rest of my life. I am so fortunate that the Advanced Bionics Harmony implant system I received is state-of-the-art and was especially researched and designed for hearing music. I was in the right place at the right time with the right need. I was able to hear the choir, though not perfectly, and there was still some accompanying ringing (which happens when the sound input is not yet well recognized by the nerves in my brain). I admit it sounded odd but I am told that it will only get better. I have a lot of hope.

While sitting in the pew I was able to share some whispered words with my daughter from time to time without my usual, "What?" and a voice so loud that everyone could hear it. That was progress. After church we went through the reception line that is accompanied by the background noise of people talking (this played as a constant ringing in my ear but not as loud as last week). I was able to have an easier conversation than the last time with the minister, who is our very dear friend, The Reverend Craig Burlington. Father Craig used to preach at my grandfather, The Reverend Francis Richey's, St. George's Church, in Maplewood, before he went to St. Luke's. At the coffee hour after the service, Sharon and I sat at a table with some other parishioners. I was amazed at how much easier it was for me to hear the folks sitting around the table. There was less strain and I felt that I was not exerting so much energy fixating on faces in order to lip-read.

So I think I passed the church test pretty well this morning and in good shape, ready to go on to meet the rest of my day. This would include a trip to Massachusetts to sit through a grandchild's ballet recital (yes, another one!) and a dinner afterwards with twelve family members at a restaurant. I did all those things in the order given. When we drove home I felt fine and was not exhausted. Yesterday I had felt "wiped out" after returning home from attending four social occasions requiring continual conversations. That was clearly too much. I collapsed on the couch *sans* processor when I returned home.

Today at church and celebrating Father's Day afterwards I had paced myself a little better with expending my energy. Perhaps the good Lord was also with me as I progressed even more into the world of the hearing. Thank you, Lord.

9

Yoga, The Dentist And French On The Beach

June 19

Yoga, the dentist and the beach: What do they all have in common? They were all places for me to discover new ways of hearing since my implant. This morning I went to my yoga class that I have not attended since pre-surgery days. My yoga teacher had always been so kind to me as I struggled to hear in her class. I knew the basic postures as I had practiced yoga for over twenty years so I was able to follow along, using my eyes as much as possible and assuming known postures. At times my teacher would alert me gently by touching my toes. Other times I might be facing in the opposite direction from the entire class. Hearing aids and reading lips weren't helping me anymore in yoga class. Had it not been for my teacher, Pam Rand, I would have given up long ago. Pam was always so encouraging and helpful. I also loved the way that yoga kept me flexible, saved my back and relaxed me so...

I continued class over the years, even as my hearing was diminishing.

I have had varied experiences with yoga classes and different teachers in the past twenty- five years since I first started yoga the summer my mother was dying. I found yoga to be a new experience and a wonderful stress release at that time. About fifteen years ago, when my hearing loss was in the severe to profound range, I went home from a class very upset because I couldn't hear anything and I wanted to take yoga so badly. I wore my assistive listening FM device in addition to my hearing aids and went back to that class and the teacher wore the microphone so I was able to participate pretty well. Then my hearing slipped to the point where FM devices did not help any more and lip reading did not work so well in the darkly lit room. I developed some coping mechanisms such as my own unique moves and postures and my teacher, Pam, would make efforts to stand near me or nudge me. Pam used to call out "Marie, can you hear me?" and I would respond, "Sometimes!" A sense of humor always helps.

Today I tried to keep myself from reading Pam's lips and looked away as I focused on listening. I have grown so used to not listening that it has become a life long habit and one that cannot be broken easily. I focused all my energy on trying to hear what Pam was saying. I heard a lot better but it was tiring. When we closed our eyes at the end of class and Pam read from a book, as she does while we are lying under blan- kets, relaxing in corpse pose, I found that I could actually hear what she was reading! I heard her read about relaxing your skin and being a part of the universe. I understood that I had been missing a lot more than I had realized in the classes of the past. Now I was gaining a whole new dimension. It brought tears of emotion to feel like a more complete part of the class.

After yoga it was time to get my teeth cleaned at the dentist. It was a different hygienist, and she walked toward the end of the room talking. Normally I would say, "Excuse me, please face me." Guess what? I heard every word she said! Amazing. Then as she cleaned my teeth and chatted I was able to follow along. When my dentist, Dr. DeSano, came in, I also heard everything he said and I could not read any lips as they were both wearing masks.

In the afternoon my friend, Dorothy, picked me up for a half-hour ride to Weekapaug, a picturesque shore area near Westerly. We were headed to visit Mary, another friend, and then we were all going to the beach. Our monthly French conversation group was going to take place at the lovely beach near Mary's old farmhouse. On the way down in the car, in spite of the wind and motor noises in the background, I was able to follow what Dorothy said. We had an interesting discussion about global warming which ended with a possible booking of her husband, a scientist, to come on my show. So many times in the past I had dreaded riding in the car with friends because I had to strain so hard to hear them and make conversation. We turned into the long, sandy driveway to Mary's eighteenth-century farmhouse. Mary came out and then gave us a little tour of her house. The three of us went down the road to the Weekapaug club beach, a peaceful strand with clean sand and clear water that is nestled among dunes, tall grass and brackish ponds. We sat on the beach together for a few hours enjoying the sun and taking swims. We spent some time speaking French and afterwards we lapsed into English. I realized that I had only said "What?" about once or twice. My face felt more relaxed and the girls told me that I looked younger (from less stress not straining to hear). They also told me that my voice had changed. This must be because I can hear myself now and I don't sound so much like a deaf person anymore. On the way back in the car with Dorothy I felt very relaxed. And to think that initially I had not wanted to go because I thought I would get too tired. I would have missed a lovely afternoon at the beach.

10

Ma Bell, Mike And Maria

Late June 2008

Why would anyone get excited about pushing a lawn mower? I did, this evening. It sounded like a lawn mower the way I knew it used to sound - loud and with a roaring engine. I was not hearing a lot of "ringing" in my ears as the lawn mower ran. To me this meant that my brain was making progress in identifying strange sounds. I happily listened as I mowed the lawn while exercising and making my yard look nicer at the same time.

I can see that I am also making big progress with the telephone. For years I have asked my assistant to make the business phone calls for me. I have not spoken to anyone I do not know on the phone for a long time. Today I called Brown University and Butler Hospital while conducting research for a show I am planning. I felt confident on the phone and my voice projected that. There was no hesitant voice that stated, "I am hard of hearing and have difficulty on the phone. Please speak more slowly." And with my follow up saying over and over again, "Would you repeat that please? Would you repeat that please?" I just sailed away on our Captel home phone, a special phone with a window to read captions, but I did not have to read the captions that I had depended upon before the surgery. I can use my cell phone also. I can hear so much better on the cell. Myron says the cell is digital and has a better sound quality.

The telephone can be a big hindrance in a hard-of-hearing person's life. It can be frightening and it can keep you from getting a job. Most professional jobs require competency with the phone. One can use the Relay Service with a special voice carry over phone or a Captel phone. But on those types of phones the hard of hearing person does not hear the other person, and it is emotionally isolating to exclude the human voice. The internet electronic mail and cell phone electronic messaging are both helpful, but there is nothing like hearing on a real phone to feel your loved one's voice or to sense attitudes in order to conduct a successful business call.

For many years I have felt cut off from the world including my family and friends because I could not use the telephone. I think it is important to compensate for things when possible so I would make sure that I saw my friends fairly often. I am a genial sort and it is important for me to socialize on a regular basis to stay balanced in life. I would make sure that I met friends frequently for lunch or tea in order to communicate in person. It has also been painful for me to struggle on the phone with one of my daughters when she wanted to have a serious conversation. I would miss every other word, especially the ones that meant something important. I felt frustrated that it was impossible to emotionally support my daughters on the phone and I am sure that they felt the same frustration.

Now that I use the phone I am so happy to be able to talk to my family again, especially to my kids and grandchildren. They call and sing silly songs and share their knock-knock jokes. I can listen to my adult daughters when they want to confide in me about their lives. It has strengthened our relationships. I can make my own business calls using my own personal style. I no longer need to rely on my assistant for matters regarding my book and television show as I have been doing the past few years. It feels liberating not to be dependent in this way.

Besides getting comfortable on the phone again I had another opportunity to practice my new hearing skills when we went with our good friends on a trip to their place in Vermont at the end of June. Mike has been my husband's closest friend since their college days at Worcester Polytech and he was the first of Myron's friends that I met. Mike used to live in the Harbor Towers in Boston right on the water and he loved to throw big parties, especially on holidays. It was a terrific view from his twenty-third-floor apartment to watch the Fourth of July or New Year's Eve fireworks. We always enjoyed our times there with Mike's friends, his hospitality and his great food.

After many years of being a bachelor around town after his divorce from his first wife, Mike met Maria in a Salsa dance class. Mike was from a conservative Jewish family and Maria from a Catholic Mexican family so they got married twice, once in the Boston Commons with a rabbi under a chuppah and another colorful Catholic wedding in a small village in Mexico, where Maria's family lives. It was an incomparable union of the brilliant, energetic Harvard business professor and the younger, refined and spirited Latin lady. They became total soul mates and they now enjoy traveling around the world as Mike delivers his seminars in Paris or Thailand while Maria explores the exotic cities. We enjoy their company very much and are happy that they found each other.

This trip to Killington with Mike and Maria would be a different experience. In the past we have always had a good time but I would have to struggle to hear all weekend and I would become very tired and possibly cranky as a result. One of the first things I noticed at their condo this time was that when I was locked in the upstairs bathroom I could hear Mike and Myron talking business outside the door. I could also hear Maria so much better with her soft voice and Spanish accent. I could hear Mike when he was in another area of the room as opposed to being two feet away on the last visit. We took a day trip to the nearby Coolidge Homestead and I could hear the guide who was taking us around and the merchants in the market. Later that evening we enjoyed a homemade gourmet dinner with wine at the condo. After dinner Mike and I sang through several verses of as many Rodgers and Hammerstein songs that we could think of. Mike said that I was singing on tune! Then we all laughed so hard until it was time to turn in. What a great new experience this was for me to enjoy being with our good friends.

11

In The Air

October 10

This was the first time that I was traveling by air since my implant and I was nervous. Besides the serendipitous case of hemorrhoids with which I had been afflicted the week before our vacation (hence the doughnut hole pillow in my bag) I would be dealing with the security system without passing through the metal detector. I had never experienced a hand-wand and pat-down security inspection before. When Myron and I arrived at the security line I learned that I would have to be escorted to the special line for medical devices. No hand-wand search there. The attendant carefully and tactfully explained that she would be doing a pat-down with gloves and did I want to go to a private place? I figured, heh, I would never see those people in the airport again, so who cares? I opted for the public pat-down. She had me spread my arms while she completed the process. It was not that big a deal. After that I could reclaim my hand luggage which held my spare processor and rechargeable batteries in one of the trays with my cosmetics. No problem there either. Then I saw Myron waiting for me off in a corner and I beamed. I had passed my first hurdle at the airport.

As I stepped out of the Providence airport at 6:30 AM and was descending the narrow steps toward the tarmac, it was raining hard. Ordinarily this would not be much of a problem, but I am not supposed to get my cochlear implant processor wet. So there I was, half awake, trying to keep moving as passengers before and behind me moved at a rapid clip. I tried to balance my carry-on, a large purse and a hot cup of coffee as I struggled to pull my jean jacket off with one hand and put it over my head. Then I was able to peek out of the small hole that appeared through my jacket and make my way about two hundred and fifty feet in the pouring rain across the slippery tarmac to the waiting plane for Kennedy airport. At Kennedy we would change for Phoenix, our destination in the Southwest to begin a two-week vacation.

Ascending the two-foot-wide staircase to the commuter plane for Kennedy with my baggage and accessories was a challenge but I made it. Then I sat down and had the surprise of my life. For the first time in all of my sixty-three years, I was able to hear AND understand every single word that the flight attendant said over the loud speaker. I was not expecting this and it threw me off guard. I listened as she requested that some passengers volunteer to get off the plane as it was too heavy so that we could take off. Fortunately, several people did so. I sat mesmerized. Then slowly tiny tears flowed down my cheeks. It was all just too overwhelming to be hearing everything.

On the way back from Phoenix a man sitting next to me offered me the use of his headset. He must have thought that I was absolutely crazy as I sat wearing the state-of-the-art headset while tears again streamed down my cheeks. I was listening to the easy music-jazz setting. Nat King Cole and his daughter were singing "When I Fall in Love" directly into my right ear. The instruments sounded so clear and I could get most of the lyrics. (In the past I could only understand one or two words, and I usually had a totally different idea of what the songs were about as my kids would sometimes translate them for me. I used to love the tune of the Beatles' song "Imagine" but I had no idea what it was about until forty years later, when I caught the lyrics in closed captioning on television and I sat on the floor and cried because the words were so beautiful.)

I leaned back in my seat and started to enjoy the long, crowded flight. I had never been able to use a headset like this on an airplane or anywhere else. One after another my old favorites came up, the ones I used to recognize by their melodies and a few key lyrics. Now I could hear almost all of the lyrics and the music was incredibly clear. This was such a gift - a sublime, spiritual bequest of the skies.

"You are So Beautiful" started to play and before that it was "As Time Goes By," other songs that I have always loved. Oh, what a wonderful world to have this beautiful music in my life! And to think that I had waited six years to get this implant because I did not want to give up music. So I continued with slightly ameliorating hearing aids and undependable lip reading to get by during the past few years. Finally I was at the right place at the right time to receive the new Harmony Bionic Ear implant. Music is more complicated to hear than speech so some of my friends who received implants a few years ago cannot hear music or else it sounds like a tin can over their ears. I was very fortunate.

Myron said that he will buy me an IPod and a good headset. Then I will be able to join the world of my grandchildren and become one of the running or walking music addicts. I can see it now: vacuuming, housework, walks in the neighborhood, waiting in train stations and sitting in planes with my favorite tunes. I am ready now, world! With beautiful music and precise notes and lyrics filling my brain I will be ready for another taste of the beauty and completeness of feeling fully alive.

12

Tea With Marie Show

February 2008

Ever since I was a little girl and went to see *The Howdy Doody Show* in person at the studio with my mother, I have wanted to be on television. Howdy Doody was a freckle-faced puppet whose friend was Buffalo Bob and enemy was Mr. Bluster. It was the only show my mother let us watch back in the early days of black-and-white television. We screamed at the top of our lungs whenever Mr. Bluster came on while Mom was fixing supper in the next room.

My first encounter with local television was when I was working at the Rhode Island Governor's Commission on Disabilities in the 1990's. I must have been in my late forties. The Commission was looking for a host for their cable television show, *Able-TOO*, and Myron said, "Why don't you do it?"

"But I have never done that before," I exclaimed.

"That's OK," Myron said, "You're a natural."

So I went and I liked it right away on the first night of taping. The director, Jeff Hartley said, "You're a natural, Marie."

It was fun. I met fascinating people and it helped me grow personally and gain confidence. The topics were disability issues in New England. I used my hearing aids and sometimes my assistive listening devices to understand the guests when interviewing them. I was always an avid lip reader so that helped. During my time on *Able-TOO*, Jeff, the director, and I became good friends and produced some other video-related projects together such as the annual Tech ACCESS of Rhode Island conferences. Once we went to Boston to film the national Self Help for Hard of Hearing (SHHH)[1] Convention, where we produced a video that was made available to hard-of-hearing individuals across the country. This video was designed to introduce consumers with what to expect at a national SHHH convention. At that convention there were some Japanese hard-of-hearing visitors whom I interviewed. They were quite a challenge with their accents and their inability to hear well.

After eight years of *Able-TOO* as a volunteer (in addition to working full time and serving on many state councils related to disabilities), I decided that I wanted to do something that had nothing to do with hearing loss. I felt that I had given fifteen years in the field of disabilities and in helping others with hearing loss. It was very satisfying but by that time I really wanted to be me, the creative side of me. I had an idea for a

[1] This organization was since renamed The Hearing Loss Association of America,

show called *Tea with Marie* and I wanted to do that. I also wanted to write a book. So I did both.

Tea with Marie was born out of my frustration with the violence and anger I saw on television, especially in our area. When the local news went from a half-hour to an hour and then added another half-hour I said to myself, "OK, that's enough of rapes, murders and fires all evening. As humans we deserve some balance in our lives. Perhaps I can do my small part in changing some of this."

I came up with an idea of having tea on the set and interviewing guests who made positive contributions to life around them. The tea idea came from my lovely southern grandmother, who took tea every afternoon at four o'clock while family and guests came to call. These tea drinkers spent the hour in pleasant conversation as they partook of the tranquil ceremony at the end of the day. My show was going to focus on "beauty, gentility and tranquility." I felt that the world could use a little more of that.

I gathered some tapes from "*Able-TOO*", a few press releases and some newspaper accounts and paid a visit to Cox communications. The director was thrilled with my idea and voila! *Tea with Marie* was born. I was thrilled too. At first I worked at a Cox cable channel in Rhode Island that produced my show. They also widely promoted the show, on every Cox cable channel, including cartoon, sports, news and other channels. Everywhere I went, to the local doughnut shops, hairdressers and pharmacies, people would say "I saw you on television!"

Little kids in the neighborhood whom I didn't know would ride by on their bikes and call out "Hi, Marie!" as though we were life-long friends. I even heard that some of the boys in the middle school were my fans. I thought this strange until I realized that the show came on after school in the afternoon and the young people were probably home alone. I started each show with "Welcome to *Tea with Marie*, we're so glad you have joined us. Please make yourself comfortable and be a guest with us as you relax and enjoy your tea." Maybe these kids were lonely and needed some company when their parents were at work. I found out that they also enjoyed the guests and the topics we had on the show. At that time in my life I remember coming home after a taping and feeling just completely and purely happy inside as I was doing something I could do (in spite of my hearing loss) and doing it well.

My show stayed on Cox channel 3 for six months and then I was told that Cox had not found any sponsors for us to continue airing so I had to go. Of course I was crushed. Little did I know that this kind of thing happens all the time in the television world. I decided to see what my next step would be. I would go back to the public access statewide channel and see if I could do a show there. This meant producing the show on my own, something I knew nothing about. But I could learn and they would train me. I had no crew, but that didn't stop me either. And of course there was the fact that I couldn't hear well, but that had never stopped me anyway. I soon found some girlfriends, mostly former teachers, and we went up to the studio for our training. Judy learned how to be a director in one session and Lesley became a camera person and later a director. Joany was a wonderful set designer, assistant producer and camera gal. Maria and Janey came on, and so it went. We were on the air for seven years and over the years, crew members have come and gone. We all learned so much and acquired new skills as well as supported each other in many other ways. We had fun and vacationed together in Florida at Judy's house in the winter.

Over the past few years *Tea with Marie* has won several PEG awards, the Emmys of the field, and we enjoyed having our work be recognized. Our guests included artists like Maxwell Mays, Mimi Sammis, Sal Mancini and Angelo Rosatti. We have had authors such as David Baldacci, Sue Monk Kidd and Ann Hood. The musicians have included David Kim, Philadelphia Orchestra Concertmaster, The Providence Singers, Joe Parillo, jazz pianist, and David Curry from Massachusetts, who leads drumming circles. Historians have included Jane Lancaster and our scientists comprised Dr. Carl Strom on global warming, Audubon staff on water and natural resources as well as medical professionals speaking about breast cancer and autism. Educational and nonprofit programs included St. Ann's Cultural Center with their unique frescoes, the R.I. Community Food Bank and The Met School. Our cooking shows included Nicole Spaulding with her French cooking lessons and Norman LeClair, former chef of The Red Rooster restaurant. Priscilla Purinton, our garden specialist, was on several times to demonstrate seasonal aspects of gardening and floral decorating. The All Children's Theater (ACT) in Providence included the youngsters who were presenting "Madeline's Christmas." As well as studio shows, we also produced many shows on location in New England including: the Newport Flower show at Rosecliff, a Japanese show in Boston, a series on old R.I. statehouses and other historic spots around Rhode Island. We were trying to make a contribution to the culture and enhancement of our world here in Rhode Island.

On the set, the crew was great about using hand signals and briefing the guests about how to talk to me so I could understand them. I have been heavily relying on lip reading for many years but this past summer my world changed. Of course, I refer to my cochlear implant. After that operation and activation I could hear my guests so much more easily. I was more relaxed and the guests could sense it. I felt more confident, less tired after taping and more challenged to search out stimulating topics for our shows with my extra energy. We produced a few shows about cochlear implants to share the information with our audience. Our show will now move into the realm of occasional documentaries as we explore worthwhile and important issues to share with our audiences in the future.

13

The Overlook Book Club

O ur Overlook Book Club was started in 1999. The club was named for the street where most of our members lived. I had put out a flyer and sent it to seven of my good friends, saying that it was "Time to have fun, read a good book and exchange ideas". At the first meeting held at my house, we discussed "Angela's Ashes" by Frank McCourt. We have met once a month since then at each other's homes. It has been almost ten years now, and we have read more than eighty books. We don't meet in the summer or December. I have a Christmas tea in December instead. We have gone on trips together, celebrated special birthdays and just grown in our friendships in general. We all look forward to it every month.

The need to start a book club grew within me as I realized that I wanted to be with good friends on a regular basis to talk and discuss interesting ideas in a milieu where I could understand. I was losing the ability to hear and to understand on the telephone and I needed a chance to connect with my friends. It is important for people who can't hear to find ways to stay connected if they are the gregarious type as I am, and don't want to be vulnerable to depression. Even so, trying to hear in a group sitting around a dimly lit living room can be a challenge to someone with hearing loss. So we established rules in our group. The first rule was to keep the club small with no more than eight or nine members. The next rule was to speak one at a time. This second rule is tough when you have a bunch of gals all getting excited about something in a book or their personal lives and everyone trying to "outtalk" each other. So we put in more rules by raising our hands and reminding people to go one at a time. For the most part, it works. We have our social hour at first and enjoy light refreshments while catching up with each other. This could be the dimly- lit- living room part where some ladies are trying to make the ambience comfy with lighted candles which is very pretty but also difficult to hear. In the second hour we get down to business and usually sit around a table where we can hear better as we discuss the ins and outs of the books we read.

There have been some funny, emotional and meaningful things that we have shared over the years together in our book club. First, I have to say that we have a wide range of ages from the fifties, sixties and a couple of feisty eighties in our club. There are equal numbers of married women and widows. No divorcees, not yet, anyway. Once we were celebrating one member's eightieth birthday and she announced to us that she had just heard from a son (none of us knew anything about him) whom she had given up for adoption in England during the Second World War. He had finally tracked her down after fifty years. I think we all had damp eyes around the table for that one. Another time we were all sitting in a circle and I guess everyone was speaking in normal voices but I, who couldn't hear, thought that they should be speaking louder. I finally lost my temper after struggling to lip read all night. I jumped up, yelled, added some curse words and implored my friends WHY wouldn't they speak up as I knew they could and WHAT WAS GOING ON? That was known as the evening that Marie lost her cool.

When our other feisty widow told us about her eightieth birthday gift from a long-lost male family friend, she had us in stitches. It seems that he had sent her eighty, that's right eighty, long-stemmed red roses for her birthday and the roses were all packed in one basket. Her daughter came over to take a photo of them. The next day the roses all dropped dead except for five of them. Ottis was devastated. She took a trip to the florist to explain what had happened and to tell them that they had not done a good job packing the roses. The florist, who had never packed eighty roses in one receptacle before — they should have divided them up, maybe? — finally relented and gave Ottis a dozen roses to make up for their error. It was an expensive error for Ottis' friend, but it was hilarious when she recounted the story.

When we read "Divine Secrets of the Ya Ya Sisterhood" we were at Ottis' house. Ottis is from New Orleans and related strongly to this book. She served us a picnic just like in the old South for our refreshments. When it was Ellie's turn to do "The "Red Tent" at her house, she built a red tent for us to sit under. Another time, Ellie, who likes to bake, had prepared plenty of yummy treats for us when we read "Just Desserts." On poetry night we read our favorite poems at Barbara's lovely home, an hour away in nearby Massachusetts and enjoyed our annual covered dish supper together. Then at my house one night we were reading "The Girl with the Pearl Earring," so of course, we were all wearing pearl earrings.

Sometimes we would take trips in Elaine's van that holds all of us, visiting Salem or Boston, Massachusetts, or other places in New England. On those occasions every one of us would become teenagers in spirit, especially Elaine and Marie, who would resort to singing in the front seat when they couldn't find their way around a town. Another time we all took a train trip to New York to see an historic exhibit about Alexander Hamilton that Ottis' son, Don Winslow, a writer, was involved in creating. We had a lovely lunch in a restaurant near the museum where we toasted each other with champagne and took the train ride back to Rhode Island later that night.

For me it was always a challenge to try to follow the book discussions or be aware of what was going on, but I usually had a good time anyway. As my hearing became worse, it would become more tiring. Therefore, I was overjoyed, as were the others in our group, when I had my cochlear implant surgery and was able to hear them so much better. I now find that I can follow the "cross table" conversation, one of the most challenging for a hard-of-hearing person in a group. I can hear in the dimly lit living rooms with the beautiful candles. I don't have to keep asking the person to my right to explain what we Sare talking about. I am noticeably more relaxed and able to focus on enjoying my friends. I am not tempted to be "paranoid" about misinterpreting what is happening around me and imagining the worst. It is a big bonus. My friends are tickled pink for me so our book club moves along more smoothly for me and everyone else now. I feel confident to contribute more of my thoughts and opinions about the books at our meetings.

The first book we read after my implant operation was "House of Sand and Fog" by Andre Dubus. This was a modern tale set in California involving an immigrant's dream and a young woman's love whose lives become tragically intertwined. We have read several books since then including Carl Bernstein's book about Hillary Clinton, "A Woman in Charge," "Water for Elephants" by Sara Gruen and the old romantic "Pride and Prejudice" by Jane Austin. One of our members enjoys the classics. At this writing our book is Ann Hood's "The Knitting Circle". Ann lives in Providence and has been a guest on my show. This novel deals with the loss of her little girl to a rare virus. We are planning "Kissing Christmas Goodbye" as light reading before Christmas to be discussed at my annual holiday tea this year. It is a pleasure to be able to discuss these books with the others in the group when I can hear what is being said.

14

Back to Naples

February 2008

These past few years I have decided that I would go south at some point during the winter to help me survive the Rhode Island weather of dreariness and dampness. I am fortunate to have some friends and relatives in Florida on the Gulf Coast. Myron doesn't care for Florida so I usually plan these trips with my girlfriends or with one of my daughters. In February 2008 I went to Naples where my sister Frani and her husband Doug live during the winter, with my youngest daughter, Joy. Joy is an attractive young woman in her thirties, 5 feet five inches tall with blond hair, blue eyes and a size two bikini, who has been a Rhode Island state trooper the past few years. She is an excellent travel companion - very easy going, flexible and with a great sense of humor. (Joy and I spent ten days on a trip together through the English countryside ten years ago and had a great time.) She is also an excellent athlete who competes with three other Rhode Island troopers in a national competition in Virginia each fall.

This year Joy and I flew separately from Providence to Southwest Florida as Joy found a cheaper ticket after I had bought mine. She has always been thrifty and clever. (When Joy was young she used to save me about $20 a week with grocery coupons and she still collects coupons for everything). The night before I left I was starting to get a little nervous about flying alone and making a transfer at Baltimore-Washington airport. Myron left me at the Providence airport curb at 6:30 in the morning for me to catch my 8:10 flight. When I turned around, he was gone, and I was on my own. When I turned around again, there was someone I knew in line behind me. Just like Rhode Island - everyone knows everybody around here. So we chatted through to the check-in and then I went over to the security line. This was my second time flying since my implant, so I knew to go right over to the side line where I stood waiting to be patted down by the TSA attendant. No problem. She did mention, however, that some people with CIs go straight through the detectors and it is not a problem. I didn't want to mess up my program but I made a mental note to check with my audiologist about this on my next appointment.

At Baltimore-Washington airport it was very easy to make the transfer. The airport was certainly cleaner and more attractive than last year, when I was stuck in a snowstorm at the dreary Philadelphia airport with my daughter, Sharon, after a trip to Naples and we had to drive back to Rhode Island on treacherously icy roads in a rental car. My confidence was gaining with each new move and I only had to call Myron once or twice to touch base. Joy and I arrived in Florida at Fort Myers Southwest airport within minutes of each other even though we had flown on different planes. Oh, the joy of cell phones for staying in touch everywhere and the joy of being able to hear on one! We headed south toward Naples in our thrifty Volkswagen rental - zipping along, chatting and laughing, an adult mother-daughter pair, acting more like two teenagers. We arrived in Naples in a half-hour with Joy's expert trooper-trained driving.

I had not seen my sister and only sibling Frani, and her husband, Doug since before my implant last summer. My sister's hearing is fine. She is a year younger but she has always acted like the older sister by being quieter, more reserved and more reasonable. I was the louder, more adventuresome and sometimes troublesome one. For some reason she made me feel nervous, ill at ease and insecure most of my adult life. I don't know if this was because of my hearing loss and if it bothered her or if her cryptic comments reminded me too much of my father. I do recall her shouting at me once when I was visiting them, "Mary, don't interrupt when Doug is talking!" When we were little there were pillow fights and I would run to my mother at times saying that "Boodie" (her nickname) was teasing me; to which my mother always responded with the old "sticks and stones will break your bones" adage. In the summers at Sagabon we had only each other to play with and I believe we did enjoy each other's company.

When we reached junior high and high school we were at different schools and had different friends and lives. Then we moved to Europe and we were together more often doing things together such as taking Berlitz French lessons and swimming in the lake the first summer, skiing at various resorts on winter holidays and attending the same class together every day at the Ecolè Nouvelle in Lausanne. One summer we sailed back to the States alone from Genoa to New York on the "Leonardo da Vinci" at the ages of seventeen and eighteen, under the watchful eye of our cabin steward and the disapproving judgment of our great Aunt Joy, who told my mother that we needed a chaperone. We had a wonderful time on that trip, laughing and drinking Spumante every night at our dining table which was filled with young people who were having the most fun in the dining room. After dinner we would sometimes sneak from cabin into first class with our friends to dance and stir things up a bit for the staid first-class passengers.

When I left Switzerland for Mary Washington College and subsequently left the college to marry Jay, my sister had to fly in from her college to be my attendant at the small wedding. My parents were still in Switzerland and I know that Frani was not happy about this situation. She did not like Jay and she did not like the idea of my leaving college. She did not smile during the whole wedding or reception. On scheduled vacations, she had to return to Switzerland and live with my parents alone, which she has related was not easy for her with our father's personality. Over the years it has been hard for me to relax around Frani. There have been several times when I have left a visit with her and unconsciously burst into uncontrollable sobs.

Finally, a few years ago I posed a question to Frani when she was visiting here, "Does my hearing loss bother you?"

"No," she said, "but your talking too much does."

Stunned at first, I gathered my thoughts and explained to her that talking too much is a typical characteristic of people with hearing loss. Then I asked her if she used e-mail because we were not having satisfactory telephone conversations ("Hi, Mary, How are you? Well that's good. Talk to you later, goodbye," type talks.) and I was feeling frustrated. After we started e-mailing each other we found a better outlet for expressing our thoughts and feelings and things have been better between us. I started to feel more a part of her life and to gain more confidence about relaxing and allowing myself to just be "me" when I visited her.

Joy and I drove up to the fashionable seaside condo complex at Naples Cay, picked up our week's guest pass at the gate and proceeded to park and unload. We rode the elevator to the ninth floor and knocked on the door of my sister's condo which faces the beach on the Gulf of Mexico. I was a little nervous but talking very strongly to myself inside about staying calm and peaceful. Boodie, opened the door with Doug following behind her. Boodie was wearing a pair of white Capri's and a chartreuse top over her slim torso and her ash blond hair was medium length in an upswept style. Doug had on a classic golf shirt and a pair of khaki pants. They both looked tan, healthy, and happy to see us. We entered the long hallway of the condo which had been redecorated recently with a gold-colored scheme and floor-to-ceiling length mirrored doors on one side that hid a door to a beige and stone-colored powder room that had an orange marble sink bowl illuminated from underneath. On the other side of the hall was a den/guest room with salmon-colored walls that was reached by sliding doors. Next to the den was the kitchen, also recently remodeled. On the last trip Myron and I had difficulty figuring out how to operate all the new appliances. The cupboards were filled with healthy food, grains and macrobiotic items. There were fresh strawberries near the sink. No cookies or sweets anywhere to be seen. Vintage wines were in the wine closet. The kitchen faced out through the living room to the large balcony overlooking the water. In the living room everything was spotless and there was no clutter or anything out of place. The new furniture was sort of a "Hemingway-esque" Key Western style with gold, yellow and green colors predominating. Boodie used a special decorator from Miami when she remodeled last year.

Boodie and Doug welcomed us with smiles and kisses and then Boodie directed us to our guest room. This was the room with the queen size bed to the right of the living room with a side balcony connected to the main balcony. The bathroom was large, full of pink marble, double sinks, a large bath tub and a glass shower. Boodie and Doug's master bedroom was on the other side of the living room. Boodie doesn't talk much but the little she said I could hear, even if she was in the other room. I didn't have to say "What?" I expected her to say something about my new hearing ability because it was such a change from years of not hearing her, but nothing came at first. That night Boodie and Doug took us out to a popular restaurant nearby. I could hear in spite of the background noise. I could answer the waitress myself without someone translating for me. I was starting to have a good time as we exchanged pleasantries about the family. We had cocktails while waiting for our light supper. Boodie and Doug spent most of the time talking to Joy about her activities. So far Boodie had said nothing about my weight. Good.

Our days at Naples that week included relaxing and taking it easy. We worked out in the mornings at the condo gym or took long walks along the beach by the smooth aqua-colored water on one side and the incredibly manicured tropical gardens of the high- rise condos on the other. Joy and I hung out by the pool and took turns sunbathing, swimming or dunking in the spa. Joy was easy company and comfortable to be with. She did talk about her love life once in a while with me and we would read our books. The living was casual. Boodie and Doug would join us for supper. One day we had my aunt over for lunch from nearby Sanibel Island where she was staying for the winter. She is ninety and seemingly the only Democrat in the Republican town of Bedford, New York. She is a "Smith-ie" with a loquacious spirit and a great penchant for discussions and debates. This time I was able to follow the conversation and inject my own political opinions as well. I started to see and hear some "other sides" of my sister and Doug as they joined the conversation with topics of their interests that I had not been aware of. I never realized Doug was such a fierce Republican and that Boodie read so many recent books.

As each day passed I found myself more relaxed and able to feel better about myself in my sister's company. I guess when you can hear what's going on around you you feel much more in control of your world and you feel like you can be the "real you" that you are. (Does this make sense?) Then you can let go of acting paranoid and pretending to know what you think people are saying about you and you can open up to a more positive interpretation of the world around you. You also tend to interrupt less and ask fewer questions that drive people crazy. Other people become more relaxed around you as a result and you can get down to the business of enjoying each other. I believe this is what took place during our visit at my sister and Doug's place. I started to stick up for myself and did not have such a "soft skin" and simply voiced my own opinions. Life worked more smoothly and simply. When it was time to leave I found that I had enjoyed my visit in Naples with Boodie and Doug and I was looking forward to seeing them again next time.

15

Rebuilding My Life

1983

After I got divorced from Jay I went to a wonderful therapist and started to rebuild my life. I did what I needed to do for myself in my new life. I needed girl-friends so I started groups to make more friendships with women. I spent time with them doing fun things such as going out to the movies and for dinner. I took care of myself and pampered myself with bubble baths and special time. I prided myself on getting the budget together and I was so excited when I got all the bills caught up to date (after many years of bill collectors calling). I was holding down a job teaching at a private school and taking care of my kids. I went to church regularly where I felt spiritual support and fellowship.

Over the years I would have my hearing tested and it would usually be about the same but then the progressive nerve loss started to worsen. I was headed into the severe range and now needed two powerful behind-the-ear hearing aids, amplification on the phone and sometimes assistive listening devices to communicate. The audiologist said that the pregnancies may have contributed to my degenerating hearing. Teaching was starting to become more challenging and I would be exhausted at night from struggling to hear the kids all day. Then one day the kids lost me on a field trip at a nearby bird sanctuary. It was a humiliating, embarrassing and potentially risky situation. This was a signal that I needed to change careers.

I called the Office of Rehabilitation Services again and this time the very wise supervisor George Bond, sent down a lovely, perfectly coiffed and groomed rehabilitation counselor named Regina Connors to visit me. Regina and I discussed what I had been doing and what skills and interests I possessed for the future. She suggested the area of counseling. When Regina left with her driver I went to my bedroom and cried. "And you are feeling sorry for yourself?" I said out loud. Regina is blind and one of the most confident, competent individuals I have ever met. Another turning point in my life: Not long after Regina's visit I registered for the master's program in human development, marriage and family therapy at the University of Rhode Island.

Before being officially admitted to the program at URI I was required to provide some experience in the clinical field. I volunteered at a crisis center in town called Sympatico. We covered everything on the emergency shift from clients who would walk in from the street with domestic disagreements to people who were suicidal and cutting their wrists in front of me while I was trying to stop the blood, calm the client and arrange admission to the nearest psychiatric facility. With amplification I was still able to work the telephone shifts there to assist those who called for help. At Sympatico I learned that helping others with their pain could help me drown out some of my own sorrows.

While pursuing my master's degree I was required to participate in an internship program. At Kent County Mental Health Center I had my first interview with the supervisor, Ellen Steinbeck, and it went something like this. I walked into the office filled with anger and defiance. Me:

"It may take me a little longer and I may be a little slower but I can do things just as well as anyone else!"

Not the best first impression.

"Marie," Ellen responded with her years of experience and understanding leading the way, "Have you ever dealt with the anger of your hearing loss?"

Another turning point: It was time for me to deal with the grief and anger of forty years of denial.

Grieving over a hearing loss is like any other kind of grief in life. As Elizabeth Kubler-Ross says, first you have the anger, then the sadness and grief before you reach the stage of acceptance. This was painful for me but it was the perfect place to take the risk. In the safe environment of the URI Marriage and Family Therapy program I had strong support. I wrote papers and revisited all those past feelings throughout my life when I was growing up and struggling to understand and be understood by family and those around me. I cried desperately and was filled with pain. I finally "got it all out" and was able to move to the other side of the mountain. There I was able to face the facts of my situation realistically and see what I was capable of doing and what I could not and plan accordingly. I felt so free when I let go and accepted that.

The Marriage and Family Therapy program at URI was a tremendous period of growth. During that time I had to work to pay bills so I put a catchy ad in the paper and started to clean houses and cater cocktail parties. I hated every moment, but I kept telling myself that it was just temporary until I would be back in the professional arena again. I especially hated it because my sister and I had inherited just as beautiful a home on Long Island as I was cleaning for others but the work helped bring in the extra money I needed for my children and me to survive. I enjoyed meeting some of the other students in the program, many of whom were around my age and struggling in their own ways. Many are still friends of mine now. I was finally doing the female friendship-bonding thing that I missed out on in junior high and high school.

After I received my master's degree I worked in the field of therapy. Then I worked in the area of disabilities in Rhode Island for about fifteen years at Easter Seals Meeting Street School, The Governor's Commission on Disabilities and TechACCESS of Rhode Island. At TechACCESS my duties included giving presentations around the state on how to use the technology available for folks with hearing loss. I was also very involved in volunteer advocacy for the deaf and hard of hearing and served on many state councils. I collected a group of deaf and hard of hearing friends and advocates in my basement that later became the Governor's Task Force and created a new commission for the deaf and hard of hearing in Rhode Island. In a sign language class at the Rhode Island School for the Deaf I learned some sign language and also met my future husband. The first night in class Myron Waldman jumped up to give me a seat when I rushed in late. Myron and I were the only hard-of-hearing students in the class. It was the first time that I had ever been involved with a man with a hearing loss. We had a lot in common and understood each other in many ways. We both became very active in the deaf and hard-of-hearing community in Rhode Island. When Myron met me he was scheduled to move to England and start a business but he changed his plans and asked me to go skiing instead. We were together for several years before we decided to get married.

Ours was an interfaith, Victorian-style wedding with a rabbi and an Anglican priest. It was held in the modest, historic South Ferry Church on a hill near Narragansett Bay. There was a sign interpreter as we had invited several deaf friends. The piano teacher played the organ. The rabbi came from Massachusetts and the Anglican priest was from nearby Kingston. Myron's Jewish relatives and friends lined one side of the church and my predominately Episcopalian guests were on the other side. Everyone dressed in their various versions of Victorian or Edwardian attire. I wore my godmother's antique Belgian lace tea gown from 1915 and Myron looked handsome in his tux with tails. Our two close friends, Ellie and Ray Fish, stood up for us. My two-year-old granddaughter, Kayla, was the flower girl dressed in an ivory satin antique child's dress from our family. She smiled as she walked bravely down the aisle. My son, Tom, led me down the aisle and proudly gave me away. Tom read from Corinthians and Myron's daughter, Sherry read The Song of Solomon. After the ceremony we went to the restaurant at Theater-By-The-Sea in Matunuck to complete our theatrical wedding with a reception. Everyone had a great time, enjoying each other, the food and drink and dancing into the night. It was my idea of the wedding I had never had the first time around and I wanted to make it special.

16

Patience with Myron

March 2008

Myron can't hear. He wears one hearing aid and struggles through each day. He wears the aid on his right ear as his left ear is totally deaf. Fortunately he can use the telephone and manages to communicate enough to conduct his business. For the past fifteen years we have both been used to not hearing well and trying to deal with that. We were involved in the deaf and hard of hearing community in Rhode Island and we were very active advocates at the state and other levels. I believe we had a kind of bond in connection with our inability to hear.

Now I can hear and Myron can't. I have to be honest, there is a conflict in me. I am so happy to be able to hear again, and even though I am not twenty-five I want to get out there and do all these things now that I can hear. I am an active person anyway, being an ENFP in the Meyers Briggs personality trait characteristics. ("E" for extrovert, "N", intuitive, "F", feeling and

"P", perceptive.) I love the theater, concerts, opera, classical music, jazz, lectures, workshops, social events and the list goes on. Myron can't do any of those things because his hearing is so limited. Why doesn't he have an implant also? Good question. We finally got him up to UMass Memorial in Worcester, where he had an evaluation with the audiologist for the cochlear implant. He failed. He is not eligible for the implant because, get this, he scored too highly on the complete sentences with a 93 percent with his right ear, the only ear he can use. Unbelievable! Yes, there are people with implants who don't even do that well, so he is not considered a candidate by the FDA and thus by the health insurance companies. He hears too well with his right ear on the test and with the other ear he hears nothing. He also has complications with calcification. But I know that he can hardly hear anything. He can't hear at social events, movies and plays. He can't hear me at home unless I am a couple of feet away, facing him and speaking in a decibel range that is not too loud (it physically hurts his ears) and not too soft (he can't hear at all). And it is hard for me to find that range, in the car, at home and most places. So much for scientific tests. We are hoping that technology and other opportunities continue to advance to help people like Myron who have profound hearing loss.

At first I felt guilty when I could hear and Myron couldn't. I wanted to shout from the rooftops about how happy I was to be able to hear all these new things and I thought that Myron would probably follow shortly after me and have the surgery too. But, no. It turns out that I am very fortunate to have such great success. After Myron was evaluated we realized that this path was not open to him. It was a real bummer driving home that afternoon from UMass Memorial in Worcester. We were both very sad. The next day we started to get back to normal.

But there are days when Myron and I get frustrated - like almost every day. First thing in the mornings we usually don't put on our hearing aid or processor so we have breakfast silently, read the paper and watch the Today Show with closed captioning. It is actually nice to greet the day without a cascade of noise - kind of like a meditation. But we say little to each other then. I read lips but Myron doesn't. Sometimes I try my limited sign language, which consists of many of my own made-up signs and I wait for several minutes until Myron responds. Kind of like a familial form of charades.

During a typical day we both go about our business with work and then we join again at supper time. This is a hectic time for most people, including young babies and children. I remember it being the "fussy time" when my kids were little. So we are a little tired and weary when preparing dinner. These are the challenging moments when Myron turns around to get a pan or walks away from me to the fridge and can't hear me. Sometimes he gets frustrated and shouts: "You know I can't hear you when" etc.

It is so easy to forget. I am trying harder to stand in front of him, speak succinctly and not say too much until we get to the table where he can hear me better. Putting a candle on the table and making dinner a special time helps us to both enjoy each other more.

Here is the conflict. To be perfectly honest and selfish, I would like to totally forget about the world of hearing loss. I actually can't remember how it was to be so hard of hearing. I know what it is like to be totally deaf when I take my processor off at night but that is just before I go to bed and fall asleep. I am so enamored of the world of hearing that I would like to totally immerse myself in it and forget my personal past struggles as a hard-of-hearing person. But I can't because I love Myron, he is profoundly hard-of-hearing and I am with him every day.

What does the Lord mean by doing this? I think it means that I am here to share with Myron and that we are a team. Even though I don't want to forcefully translate for and embarrass Myron by taking the lead in communication, I know I can be of help to him in many situations, such as when we are traveling and socializing. I will just have to keep on practicing patience with him every single day and focus on those good things that we share, for as my wonderful mother used to say, "Patience is a virtue, my dear."

Those words were helpful preparation for me now when the Lord is working in a mysterious way.

17

Family Members

April 2008

Communication can make or break a relationship. Imagine what it can be like for someone who can't hear most of what goes on and is trying to get along with her new daughter-in-law or stepdaughter. I don't have to imagine as I know what that is like.

Eleven years ago my son was married to a beautiful young lady from Chicago. The family as well as guests from over twenty countries went out to Chicago for the weekend of wedding festivities. It was a lovely wedding in a large cathedral followed by a reception in the Intercontinental Hotel with the best band in Chicago playing. We danced until one a.m. and had a fabulous time. My son, Tom, had met his bride, Sara, at a friend's wedding in our town of Narragansett and now they were getting married where Sara's family lived. Families were gradually being combined with the numerous rituals that occur at weddings. There were pre-wedding parties, showers and opportunities for sharing stories, jokes and viewing photos of the couple as children. It was a jolly affair. Then Tom and Sara moved to Rhode Island and eventually had a family of three children of their own.

Tom and Sara only live about twenty minutes away from here, the closest to me of any of my children. From the start I found it a blessing to have them nearby, but I was not always comfortable baby-sitting for the children. I finally told my son that I loved his kids but could not hear them that well; I felt conflicted as I wanted to be with them but I was concerned about "losing" them in their large house when I couldn't hear them. I actually did lose Drew once and went all over the house upstairs and down looking for him. I would go to baby-sit from time to time but not as often as I would have wished. Children grow up quickly. I was very fortunate that I had my implant and now I can go to visit or babysit Tom and Sara's kids and hear their little voices and understand them. I am much more comfortable, and the kids seem more at ease around me also.

I also feel more comfortable with my daughter-in-law, Sara, whose voice and pattern of speech I had some difficulty understanding for many years. Sara is a petite, attractive brunette who recently turned forty. She is very committed to raising her children as Tom is away during the week on business and it is Sara who takes care of all their needs and taxis them to all of their sports, ballet and play dates. When Sara has a spare moment, which is rare, she enjoys running and physical activities such as yoga and working out. She is a social worker by profession and when she was first married and lived in Chicago she used to go to work in some of the most challenging areas of Chicago. For many years I had a hard time communicating with Sara as she tends to speak rather quickly and I could not understand her. She used to have Tom speak to me on the phone for her, when I was still able to use the phone some years ago, because she felt uncomfortable not knowing if I could hear her or not. Now we email each other and use the phone occasionally. Sara says that she feels like I am understanding her better and it makes her feel more comfortable. I am trying to be more attentive to her needs after we have had several honest conversations together this past year. These conversations usually involved things going on in our family and sharing our different opinions so that we could understand each other better. Some how it was hard to have honest conversations when you would miss a word here and there and couldn't always understand a new member of the family. It was easy with my own kids because they knew my ups and downs and accepted me as I was but I wasn't sure about my children's spouses who had not grown up with me. Now Sara and I are finding out all kinds of things about each other and I am enjoying my relationship with her more and more as we discover things we have in common, such as certain authors and books, foods, recipes and hobbies. This is all because I am better able to communicate with her and she feels more at ease.

Since Myron and I are a combined family (he has four adult children and I have four, and we each have seven grandchild dren) there are many dynamics in the various relationships. One of his daughters, Sherry, and her husband, Michael, would come to visit and I would have a very hard time hearing them as they tend to speak quickly and softly and sometimes even mumble. As a result of this, I might find myself not saying anything or I would activate the "deaf nod" while I completely missed the conversation. I was not very comfortable as I felt left out of the conversation and unable to state my point of view honestly. This would lead me to becoming nervous and a little paranoid when around them as I did not know them that well and could not hear the jokes or share repartee with them. Now that I can hear better I find myself more at ease with them and their children and enjoy their visits so much more. When the young children, Eliana and Katrina, come for visits now, I can sit around the table at dinner and share imaginative conversations with these interesting, creative kids. I am learning from them and I think they are learning something from me.

What can I do now that I couldn't do before my implant with my family? Well, for one thing, I don't dread those family sitting-around-the-table-moments or family standing-around-the-island-in-the-kitchen times. At those times I used to feel completely left out and could not understand any of the cross conversation at all. It would be just about impossible, also, at a cruise dinner, with Myron's family on a ship while we were all vacationing together. On one cruise I lasted about half way through the dinner and then begged to excuse myself. I went back to my cabin with a headache from straining to hear and had a good cry as I regressed into my childlike mode of feeling lonely and neglected. I am now looking forward to the next cruise with Myron's family. I hope there is one!

Here's what happens now at family get-togethers when there is a lot of conversation going on. I am much more relaxed and don't feel that dread that I might not hear anything and be left out. I can smile more often and understand the cross conversation and overlap that goes on when people get together and enjoy each other's company. I am learning more about and taking more of an interest in the opinions of others in the group such as those of my daughter and son-in-law. My son-in-law, David, and I can joke and kid around more together and I can understand more about his work and career. And who knew my brother-in-law, Doug's political opinions? I can now include my own political opinions and take a stand. I don't speak "over" people or interrupt as much because I can hear and I am willing to listen more and wait more patiently because I don't have those strong feelings of being left out. True, I am training myself to listen more, as sixty years of bad habits can take a while to change.

Family events, such as a recent funeral I attended, are much less stressful for me in communication. I can hear the rabbi or minister in the pulpit and don't have to ask my neighbor for a translation. At the reception after the funeral of one of Myron's relatives recently I was able to listen and not nod into oblivion and I could actually conduct appropriate and accurate conversation. (There is nothing like getting it wrong at a funeral and saying something like, "Oh isn't that nice," after someone has told you his relative has died.) At a recent trip to the symphony in Providence I was able to chat effortlessly with family and friends during the intermission in a very noisy hall and even make a few jokes and laugh. I am a happier person in general. I am also becoming a much more informed person as my resources extend wider than the written word or captioned television (I am now realizing that closed captioning is not always completely accurate). Listening to the public radio broadcasts in the car is keeping me more informed of recent events.

Many factors have changed within my family dynamics and within me since I had my cochlear implant activation less than a year ago. As family events and activities unfold I find myself enjoying more and more of them while my world is expanding and the opportunities to share happy memories with my family are becoming more numerous.

18

The Garden

April 2008

I am in the garden; at least I seem to be. Here in the corner of my sun-room where I now keep my computer and a few desk belongings I find I can write more easily than in my well organized, though isolated and somewhat depressing office in the basement. The reason is because I can look out as I am doing, on this warm sunny April day and see the brilliant forsythia bordering my property and the green clumps of Japanese iris pushing their heads up through the ground. I can hear the mating songs of the various birds with their eternal calls to each other and I am starting to learn the difference between a robin and a sparrow's voice. Each day the different trees provide their softly painted leaves of new light green and the bright pink of the Japanese plum tree just opened today. It is spring and almost a year since my cochlear implant operation last May.

As a child, I remember my mother in the garden on Long Island in the summer and in New Jersey during the spring. I remember my grandmother also, as she walked around her rose garden bordered by boxwood, in high-heeled shoes with a long dress and jewelry around her neck. She was around eighty when I knew her, and although she took much joy in it, she could only walk around the garden that someone else, perhaps my mother, had prepared. It was my mother whom I remember kneeling in the dirt with a trowel in her hand, wearing an old denim smock, with her long auburn hair piled loosely on her head under a cotton kerchief and with a serene smile on her face. As a child I used to wonder why on earth my mother would work in the garden for what seemed like forever and ever to me. When I called her she would respond, "Just a few more minutes, dear, a few more minutes."

And finally, it has been I, saying to my children, while they were growing up, "Just a few more minutes, dear," or to my husband, Myron, now, "Just a few more minutes, dear" as I try to stay outside until seven p.m. while he is getting impatient for his dinner. How can I explain those feelings that I have while in the garden? They are probably the same ones my grandmother and mother had as well those that my daughter, Dawne and son, Tom, now have. To be in the garden when the sun is shining and the first fresh days of spring have burst forth after a long cold winter is like paradise. I have unlocked the secret of my mother and the agrarian sisters before her. I have found the key to contentment and tranquility as I lose myself totally in another consciousness, one with the earth and its beauty surrounding me as well as the endeavor to create more loveliness.

Perhaps the garden has been my sanctuary over the years. Since the days of my first marriage, when we bought this plain ranch house sitting on a parcel of land thirty-five years ago, I have been constantly at work every spring to define it, embellish it and transform it. This includes the times when I battled with the land by trying to mow the lawn with sore legs, was bending over it with a bad back and abstaining from it the summer I contracted Lyme disease. My mother was the first to visit our new home, bearing fragrant wild rose bushes to define the corners of the until-then-un-baptized premises. At that time I was too burdened with babies and had neither the time nor interest in the garden. Mother planted the rose bushes and then brought the Japanese iris, day lilies and Rose of Sharon from Sagabon on various trips. She also brought the lavender lilacs, the last remnants of the Sagabon lilacs. Sagabon has long since been sold many times over to wealthy New York show business magnates, but the Sagabon lilacs remain in my garden as well as in my son's, daughter's, neighbor's and friends', a testimony to my childhood memories.

Over the years through a troublesome first marriage, raising four children, returning to college, careers pursued alongside motherhood, my own kids going off to college and eventually a new and fulfilling marriage, in the springtime I have always found the haven in the garden. It was similar to the concept of asylum I have been experiencing when I found I could hear after having been hard of hearing for so long. Now I am able to hear so many different things outside and not all of them depict the overall effect of a peaceful garden. There are the sounds from beyond my garden, such as dogs barking, loud parties, airplanes and the distant roar of cars on the highway and motorboats on the river. But then there are the sounds of nature, far outweighing the modern noises in my mind. In the spring I notice that the birds are singing louder and perhaps more joyfully, especially early in the morning. In the garden are birdbaths and bird feeders to encourage my feathered friends. Even though my son (the ornithology expert) tells me he does-n't feed the birds in the late spring, I offer thistle seed (to discourage the squirrels, who eat all the regular bird seed) and for my own enjoyment, so I can watch and listen to them. Now I enjoy hearing them splash in their baths as well as watching them.

We have had an exceptional April this spring and it would be so tempting for me to ignore everything else in my life and stay outside in the garden. But this cannot be done. I must come in and do my work and my writing. My husband has been rea-sonably patient when dinner is late. I must also watch my sore back and conduct myself with moderation. Carefully, I find myself now, working in the garden, under the sun, one with the birds as I call out to them and they answer me, a mature woman, a mother and a grandmother with new hearing, who is finding even more joy in her beloved garden.

19

At the Theater

May 2008

As a young person when I lived in New Jersey my favorite thing was to go to the theater on Broadway in New York City. During my teen years Mother would get me tickets in the first row where I could hear, for many special occasions, such as birthdays. I was fortunate enough to see the original "My Fair Lady," "Music Man," "West Side Story," "Sound of Music" and "Cabaret," among other musicals. My mother or my sister and I always had a great time. My love for the theater was so great that my Mom took me to Stella Adler and The American Academy of Dramatic Arts in New York while a teenager to check them out. I knew I would have trouble hearing there, however, so I did not pursue those schools, even though the director of Stella Adler was impressed with how I concentrated on his face. (I was lip reading.) I did participate in talent shows and dance recitals in my high school. In tenth grade I gave my interpretation of Edo Annie from "Oklahoma" while singing and dancing in a skit I impro-vised to "I Can't Say No." A perfect part for an active teenager! I also used to go around the house singing all the Rodgers and Hammerstein songs, which my mother said were "lovely, dear, even though you sing an octave lower than anyone else." Mom was just glad to hear me singing and spreading happiness.

Throughout my life I have enjoyed the theater but struggled to hear the dialogue. I usually preferred musical comedies with songs, dances and visual enhancements. Last year I was able to see one of my granddaughters, Callan, portray Madeline in "Madeline's Christmas" at the All Children's Theater in Provi-dence. She was ten and just starting to participate in theater. She had the "bug." Then my eldest granddaughter, Kayla, became interested and soon she was "Into the Woods" as Cinderella the last year in her middle school in Massachusetts. Even though I could not hear them well, I was very proud of both my granddaughters and enjoyed watching them do such a great job.

This year it is such a different experience to enjoy theater. Kayla had the lead in "Seussical" and played The Cat in the Hat. What a joy it was to see and hear her singing, dancing, acting and being comical in her role as the cat. Her extended family took up a whole row in the large auditorium and we all had a great time. The little four and five-year-old girls were wide-eyed as they leaned forward in their seats throughout the performance. I was able to hear most of the dialogue, probably about 75 to 80 percent, which is much better than 0 percent from before my implant. It was also a lot of fun to watch four-teen-year-old Kayla sign autographs after the show for the little children. I was happy for her and the experience she was having and I was definitely living vicariously through her.

I heard from Trinity Repertory Theater in Providence that they were going to provide captioning for deaf and hard-of-hearing people at their theater in Providence just as the theaters on Broadway and around the country are starting to do. The first captioned performance in Rhode Island would be "Blithe Spirit" by Noel Coward. Naturally, I had to invite Curt Columbus, artistic director at Trinity, and Randall Rosenbaum, executive director of the R.I. State Council on the Arts, supporter of the captioning equipment, on my show, *"Tea with Marie."* It was a good show and we had a chance to talk about the theater and the need for accommodation for folks with disabilities and what was now available around Rhode Island. When Myron and I went to see "Blithe Spirit" at Trinity we were so excited. There were the large red letters of the captioning at one side of the theater in a sign inauspiciously hanging in the air in front of the many deaf and hard-of-hearing theater-goers. Myron was thrilled as he can't hear anything at a theater, and I was glad to have some help with the British accents of the actors in that particular play.

These types of accommodations available at theaters around the country for deaf and hard-of-hearing people make it possible for many to enjoy the theater who might otherwise stay home and miss out. It is not fair to stay home and miss out. After a few times of missing out it is easy to not feel like going anywhere and that's when one can become prone to depression

and other difficulties. Deaf and hard-of-hearing people, especially outgoing ones need to have the same opportunities as
others to get out there in the world and enjoy what's available.
Theater offers people an opportunity to come out of themselves
and discover other points of view as well as simply enjoying the
entertainment.

Now that I have my implant I am not too embarrassed to
make another debut of my own in the theatrical sense, during
my "mature years." That is why I am going to do a song and
dance number from "Cabaret" in our church talent show. After
all, once a ham, always a ham, only this time the ham has a
better chance of singing on tune!

20

Music, Music, Music

May 2008

As a young girl with a moderate hearing loss I could hear well enough to listen to my father practice his songs. He used to sing "Bill Bailey Won't You Please come Home" and "Sometimes I Feel Like a Motherless Child" for his New York City University Glee Club concerts as he shaved in the bathroom in the morning. My father was the main musical focus in our family. What do you expect? He was from Austria. When I was very little he used to play the accordion as well as sing. He also sang in the church choir. In fact, listening to beautiful choir music such as "Lo How a Rose E'r Blooming" and "Slumber Song of the Infant Jesus" was a big part of our family's Christmas celebrations. Even if I couldn't hear all the lyrics, I loved the sweet melodies.

While I was growing up in New Jersey, we lived in an old Victorian house filled with the sounds of the Texaco Opera reverberating through the rafters every Saturday afternoon. As my hearing loss was in the moderate range then and I could not understand the foreign languages, I still felt the emotional impact of the music. Saturday afternoons were special in our home. At the end of the opera, after my father had finished working on a remodeling project around the house and my mother had completed her chores they would sit down together for tea and a bite of that delicious Danish almond coffee cake from Peter's bakery in the village. I loved that coffee cake and I loved those peaceful moments.

Guess what I have been doing this past winter? Listening to the Metropolitan Opera live from New York on my FM radio station on Saturday afternoons. What a different experience it is now with my cochlear implant because, as I have mentioned earlier, I have a recent model processor (the Advanced Bionics Harmony) that was researched and designed especially for better understanding of music. I can even understand some of the lyrics and dialogue in operas such as "Carmen" and "La Fille du Regiment" (so much fun to practice my French). This is one of my favorite moments in the week: to have the opera filling my head while the warm sun light filters through my body as I relax in the sun-room with a cup of tea, after having finished my work on a Saturday afternoon. Sometimes Myron joins me and we have our tea and coffee cake together.

In Europe I was privileged to attend classical concerts in Lausanne and Paris. Our parents would take my sister and me to many of the musical events that came to Lausanne from around the world. In Paris there was a cultural program as part of our college activities and we often went to the Paris Opera or to concerts at The Salle Pleyel and other concert halls with our student passes. My hearing at that time was enough to appreciate the melodies of the music but not the lyrics of the songs. It was during the early sixties and the Beatles were starting to come on the scene and later the folk singers of the peace movements. I remember hearing the songs and enjoying the catchy tunes but not understanding the lyrics.

I have mentioned that I used to love to sing around the house while growing up, especially Rodgers and Hammerstein. I didn't care if I got all the words right. I just loved to sing because it made me happy. When my children were growing up we had lots of parties around our house with singing being part of the festivities. Once we had a block party in our driveway and I surprised some of our neighbors by dressing up in an evening gown and booming out to the street filled with children and adults, "I Could Have Danced All Night" from "My Fair Lady." It was a joyful performance and no one held it against me. In fact, it broke the ice and I met some new neighbors who have been good friends ever since.

Maybe that is one of the reasons that I wanted to sing on my sixtieth birthday a few years ago. No one likes to turn sixty, so I was looking for something to do that would be a little crazy but not dangerous. I decided to invite all of my friends and family to a local cafe where I would act as the emcee and I would also sing four songs that I would learn. This was "Before Implant Operation" so my singing abilities were limited at best, but I was determined. I went to the nearby University of Rhode

Island and took a couple of singing lessons in the music department and then I went to have a forty-five-minute session with the pianist/accompanist who would play for me that night. The only gift I wanted for my birthday was the opportunity to pretend I was on Broadway, my childhood dream, and have my friends and family be my captive audience.

Myron introduced me at my party and then said a few kind words. I took the stage with "The Sound of Music." I explained how I had been told all my life that I could not sing and that recently a singer on my show had said that I had a nice voice (maybe not always on tune but a nice quality) and I was going to give it my all as I sang into my sixties. I also sang "Try to Remember" and "Climb Every Mountain." The big hit was the song I sang in French, "Le Bleu de L'Eté," or "The Green Leaves of Summer". Some thought I sounded like Edith Piaf. I think it was because they couldn't understand French. I closed the show with a quote from Goethe, since the theme was "Following Your Dream." Goethe reminds us "Whatever you can do or dream you can do. Begin it. Boldness has genius, power and magic in it."

My sixtieth party included other musician friends who added to the fun, including a troupe of energetic professional African drummers from Mali, friends of my daughter's. It didn't seem to matter how well one heard when we were all dancing wildly to the drum beats from Africa and feeling the vibrations. Even Myron danced furiously. In fact, we all had such a good time that we decided to repeat the celebration for a few years in a row as a "Mid Winter Music Blast" at The True Brew Café.

During this past year I have been practicing singing by listening to the good singers next to me in church and trying to mimic them. My daughter, Sharon, inspired me after she told me that it was the first time she had ever heard me sing in tune at her church after my implant. When I sang with my church choir one day the other choir members said that I was doing fine and did not throw anyone off key (I asked them). So it came as a surprise to me when I went to practice with someone in my church who was to play the piano for me while I sang and danced "Cabaret" for a talent show. She told me that I could not carry a tune and that it was "pretty bad." She did add that she did not want to hurt my feelings. I said not to worry, I would manage something.

"Maybe you should lip sync or just dance to a tape and not sing," was another suggestion she gave me. After I left her place I thought to myself, "Why had no one told me that before?"

Everyone knew that I was hard-of-hearing a few years ago on my sixtieth birthday and it did not seem to be a problem. No one complained of ears hurting. It seemed that everyone at True Brew Café had a lot of fun. When I went home I did feel hurt after all.

I decided to go ahead with the act anyway and keep my spirits up and not let someone talk me out of it because it is a part of me to sing and listen to music. If I did not hurt anyone's ears then I was not giving up singing and expressing this joy in my life. A good friend and neighbor of mine, Elaine, said that she would sing and do the routine with me for the talent show and we would have fun and try to help others enjoy themselves. Elaine came over and we only had a few days to practice together. Elaine was having a hard time learning her lines. We dressed up in our costumes with sequins, top hats and lots of "bling" and grabbed some hiking poles for our canes to wave around like they used to do in vaudeville. We went to the church and asked the emcee to bill us as the first act. We lined up side by side, with our hats held high in the air and Myron started to roll the camcorder. Then we went into our routine. We started singing and dancing and when we came to the end of the first verse, Elaine couldn't remember her lines. The audience laughed. A bit later there was a place where neither of us could remember a certain line. We hesitated and stared at each other. The audience laughed again. Elaine started to ham it up and I followed suit. We were like George Burns and Gracie Allen in a song-and-dance act. At the end the audience gave us a standing ovation. The next day in church, a choir member said, "Marie, who knew you could sing! You'll have to join the choir."

I think I might even take singing lessons in the future because, after all, I am not one to give up easily.

21

Listening To Oprah

May 2008

Oprah Winfrey is my mentor. She doesn't know it but my dream is that she will some day. As I meet guests for my television show I find more and more of them also have dreams to appear on Oprah's show. That's OK. It is important to have a dream. But, seriously, I learn a lot from Oprah and I find it very helpful as the host on my show, "*Tea with Marie.*" The main thing I have learned from Oprah is to be myself. When I stop trying to please others in a way that I think they want me to and just relax and am me, Marie, I find that I am more relaxed and my guests tell me that they are also. We have a comment book where guests can share their thoughts about being on our show. We get comments about how gracious our crew is and how comfortable the guests feel being interviewed. Everyone should relax and be themselves because that is the natural way and that's what makes the world so diverse and interesting.

I work out of my home and I write in my sun-room where I can see the flowers outside in the summer, geraniums and begonias blooming inside in winter and birds all year long. Many times after I have spent the day writing or at my computer I find myself turning on the television around 4 p.m. and checking to see what Oprah is doing. If she has something I find interesting such as a philosopher, author or viewer with a unique story I make myself a cup of tea and settle in to watch. Sometimes my friend, Elaine, from across the street comes over to watch Oprah with me.

Over the past thirty years Elaine and I have shared many adventures together. We have done everything from starting a play group in my basement that developed into a licensed local nursery school, to selling coffee at 6:00 AM (after waking at 5 to brew the coffee and then drive twenty minutes away to buy the doughnuts) to cars in lines for the gas stations during the gas crisis in the seventies. As good friends, it seems as though Elaine and I have been through so much. We were single divorcees and then we got remarried to better men. We saved each other's lives in the middle of the night when the ambulances came. Together we shoveled three feet of snow on our driveways during the great blizzard of '78 as we listened to the portable radio on the hood of the car where Ron, Elaine's husband, who was stuck in Providence, was narrating the news on WEAN radio. We've been through times when we have spoken to each other and times when we have not spoken to each other. We are in the same book club and we go to the same church. Most of all, Elaine and I do a lot of laughing together and that always makes us both feel better. So Elaine comes over and sometimes we watch Oprah and we laugh a lot.

From Oprah we learn about fashion, clutter, nutritious food, the human body, sex, our health and many psychological issues. Before I could hear better I used to watch Oprah by reading the closed captioning that runs on the bottom of our television screen. Now I can hear and understand and have no more need for the captioning. It is incredible. If I miss a name, however, the captioning can come in handy. Recently my husband and I have been following Oprah's web cast classes live on ten Monday nights with Oprah and Eckhart Tolle. It has been a joy to actually sit in front of the computer screen and listen to Oprah and Eckhart and understand every single word they say. I am learning all about "The New Earth" and how the "pain bodies" can creep up on you but if you stay in your awareness and stage of presence it won't happen so often and when it does you can handle it better. I am realizing that Oprah has a penetrating intelligence as she summarizes and adds her own perspective to Eckhart's on this live broadcast. It is incredible to hear the questions from viewers around the world who are listening and trying to learn how to live a more peaceful life by using some of Eckhart's ideas. All this I am learning because I can hear again! How exciting this is and how I must never take this for granted.

As well as listening and understanding Oprah, which adds to my world and expands my awareness, I find that when I am in my car I can turn on the radio and listen to NPR, National Public Radio. I could never understand talk radio before my

implant. Now I can comprehend every single word. How fascinating it is to hear the BBC perspective of the world news or
the interviews with the writers and screen writers. I am ab-
sorbing more in-depth stories about politics and world affairs.
Sometimes it is a bit much to handle and becomes overwhelming so I take a break and go back to my classical music station.
It does feels good, however, to be able to contribute more in
conversations because I have heard some of the information on
the radio or on television from people like Oprah and others.
My perspective is enlarging and I am feeling more intelligent
and more worthwhile as a person with valuable opinions who
is not afraid to express them. In this regard, Oprah is someone
I can really appreciate.

22

Hearing In French

May 2008

When I was fourteen I made my first trip to France. My mother took my sister and me with her to spend the summer there the year after her father died. We stayed with my aunt and uncle (my father's brother) and their family of two children in Aix Les Bains, an ancient spa town near the Lake du Bourget in Savoie in the French Alps. There are still remnants form the Roman baths and today guests can go to "take the waters" there. It is about an hour southwest from Geneva, Switzerland. Tante Simone taught my sister and me French lessons every morning. Whenever we did anything with Tante Simone she would teach us French words. When we made the long walk to the beach on the lake in the afternoons she would say, "Nous allons a la plage maintenant."

My sister and I had a lot of fun that summer and everything seemed so strange to us, the house, the food, the customs and, of course, the language. We watched Tante Simone go to the market every morning to search for bargains for the day's meals and saw how she managed without a refrigerator (she kept the butter and cheese on a cool, shady shelf in the back of the kitchen).We took sponge baths because there was no bathtub in the house, ate our main meals in the middle of the day and had delicious soups and *salade verte au vinaigrette* at night (my aunt was an incredible cook).The adults drank wine with each meal and mixed a little of the *vin du table* with water for *les enfants*. But there was one thing that was not unusual. What was not strange for us was the music in 1958. My cousin, Marie Thé just loved American music. So did we. We spent many hours listening to and dancing to Elvis Presley, Pat Boone and "Les Platters." In fact one of the highlights of our summer was to go to the beautiful white marble Casino in town one evening and hear "Les Platters" sing and chat with them afterwards (in English) as we collected their autographs.

Tante Simone would not allow my sister or me to walk through the town without a chaperone so either she, my cousin or my mother would accompany us. My cousin was only four years older, so it was more fun when she was with us. We walked all over the pretty tree-lined town, saw the Roman baths where people went to "take the cure" or just take a bath (not everyone had bathtubs in their homes then). My cousin loved ballet and was a good dancer. She introduced me to my first French boyfriend, Jean Pierre, who was a ballet dancer at Marie Thé's dance school. He was tall, dark and very hand-some. I thought I was desperately in love. Marie Thé and her boyfriend and Jean Pierre and I would take lots of walks around the surrounding mountains. I always carried my little Berlitz book with me so we could communicate. I would simply point to the English sentence and Jean Pierre would read the French. I believe that our conversations were rather limited.

The next time I went to Europe was when we moved there as a family in 1961, the year I was going into my senior year in high school, as I have recounted earlier. Since my small classes were in French at my high school, Ecolè Nouvelle de la Suisse Romande in Lausanne I had a great opportunity to learn the language, even with my hearing loss. The male teacher's voice was large and booming. Living with a French family in Paris gave me more opportunities to pick up French and the colloquial expressions at the time as well as become acquainted with French culture.

I have a great affinity for all things French. I also have French Huguenot ancestors and my mother was a complete Francophile. Perhaps that is why I decided to take some French classes at a nearby library a couple of years ago. The class was filled with adult students from all walks of life with various levels of ability in speaking and understanding French. There were only a few who could speak proficiently. I sat near the teacher, using my assistive listening device amplification system along with my hearing aids and lip reading to manage in her class. By the end of the class the teacher said "See you next month" and gave us some homework in the high school level reader we were assigned. There had not been much time for conversation in the class. Just at that moment a lady to my right-nudged me (I think she was reading my mind). "Would you like to meet more frequently for French conversation?" she asked. I answered, "oui." We found a few others and soon we were meeting at each other's houses (and sometimes the beach). We started our meetings two years ago, before my implant, when I was desperately trying to read lips to keep up with this small group, but we had a good time and the women were an interesting bunch. Because Rhode Island is so small, one of the ladies in the group turned out to be my granddaughter Callan's teacher at her private school.

Since I received my implant I have been meeting with my French-speaking friends during the past year and I would say that my ability to hear in the group has improved 100 percent. I hope my French has! We are fortunate to have one woman in our group who is from France, and she gently corrects us so that we don't speak poor French over and over to each other. Very soon we will be taking a trip to visit my cousin, Marie Thé, for her son Hervé's wedding in France. Myron and I are looking forward to this trip. I am hoping that now that I can hear so much better I will catch on very quickly when I am immersed in the French language during all the festivities and start speaking French again like a pro.

23

On The Road

May 2008

We live in the southern part of Rhode Island affectionately called "South County" by the locals even though no such place actually exists. The official county name is Washington, after our first president, who seemed to travel back and forth across this area on his way to Newport or Boston looking for money to support the Revolutionary War. It is a somewhat rural area of villages scattered through woods bordered by stone walls and flanked by the Atlantic Ocean on the east and Connecticut on the west. To go grocery shopping or get to the dry cleaners or hospital you have to travel about fifteen or twenty minutes. Even to get from one end of suburban/rural Narragansett to the other takes about twenty-five minutes. In other words, you need to use your car. There are buses but they don't always go where you want to go, but I am sure that will be changing as oil prices continue to go up.

We have a hybrid that my husband has driven since they first came out and I drive a small SUV type of car. Someone once asked me recently, "How is it driving when you can't hear very well?" I told her that I use my eyes a lot and constantly check the rear-view mirror and side mirrors and try not to speed, especially in certain places. Driving seems a lot safer now with my implant. Before that I had a few adventures. I remember once when I was racing to work, running a little late, from Narragansett to East Providence, where I worked at Easter Seals Meeting Street School about fifty minutes away. I had the radio on and suddenly I realized that a policeman was behind me so I pulled over. He said that he had been tailing me for a while and that he had his lights flashing and siren on. "Oh, dear, Officer," I said, (realizing that my hearing must be getting pretty bad as I was unable to hear much outside of the car when I had the radio on)." I am trying to get to work and I don't want to be late or I might be fired." I must have looked very forlorn because the kindly state police officer asked for my license and then said, "Well, you are lucky today as we are having a special on two things and I see you have your seat belt on so that is good." He didn't mention the other thing but simply said that he wanted me to be safe and to have a good day. Whew! I thought I was lucky. I had not realized how bad my hearing was becoming so from then on I was more diligent about using my eyes to watch out for policemen and other possibilities.

As my hearing became worse over the past few years I found it became more difficult and required much more energy to converse with others in the car. By this time I was relying on lip reading and it was a tricky maneuver to drive and read the lips of my passengers at the same time. It was a particular challenge to drive and try to read the lips of those in the back seat or at night. In fact I obviously could not do that in the dark. It would be daytime when I would drive the girls on the crew up to the studio to tape the show but when we drove home at night I could not follow a word so I would sit silently for an hour and feel very left out of everything. I recall instances where I had to sit in the back seat of cars or taxis with people I did not know well or guests I had just met and feeling so frustrated. I could not hear them and would be too embarrassed to tell them because I did not know them well or I was obligated to converse with them.

Before my operation I could hear the classical music station when it was turned up very high. I could not understand talk radio at all. So imagine my surprise when I put on National Public Radio a few weeks after my activation for my implant and could hear the conversation. I now turn on NPR the minute I get in the car and I enjoy learning so much more about the world. I find that I am more confident about expressing my opinion about politics or news-worthy events since I have been able to include some information from NPR that I have tucked into my brain. Sometimes I get tired of hearing about the disasters in the world and change the channel back to music but I do like listening to the authors, screenwriters and other fascinating commentators.

One of the delightful aspects about riding in the car now is being able to hear my little grandchildren who sit in the back seat. In the past when I would pick them up from their homes and drive a half-hour or an hour away to where I live I would not be able to chat with them or answer their questions. Sometimes I would tilt the rear-view mirror to read their lips and a few times we tried the assistive listening devices but they were not always helpful. The other day I was driving my eleven-year-old granddaughter, Callan, back to my house and she was going on and on about the kids in her class and the books she liked to read when I realized how great it was to talk with her back and forth as I had understood everything she said. We both mentioned to each other what a nice change that was. It made us feel like we were a part of each other's lives.

The automobile can be a challenging setting for a person with hearing loss for many reasons: the noise of the wind, the motor, the air conditioning and other cars and trucks going by. Background noise is difficult for folks wearing hearing aids. I once had to take a car back to the dealership because it was too noisy and buy another that was quieter. The technology of my implant is different from the hearing aid and does not give me problems with background noise in the car or most other places. Now I look forward to jumping in my car when I have to go on errands around South County and other places because I can turn on talk radio, find out about what is happening in the world and feel a part of what is going on around me. I can also feel more comfortable when I am riding in the car with friends or people I have just met.

24

What I Thought I'd Never Hear And Sounds Of Silence

May 2008

D iscovering things that people talk about in public has been a new learning experience.

There are the folks speaking on their cell phones, parents dragging their kids through supermarkets and young people playing ball at the beach. When I first started to hear these conversations I felt like I was eavesdropping. One day at the beach nearby, I heard a mother scream out, "You lazy little kid, get out of the water right this minute or I am going to go over and drag you out." I thought to myself: "I'm not supposed to know how this woman is treating her child." l felt awkward and uncomfortable.

I heard a husband and wife arguing about what kind of potting soil to buy in the hardware store.

"It's not a bargain if it isn't good quality," said the wife. The husband countered with how they were going to buy two bags of that brand and two bags of the other and that was settled. I recognized in that moment that many couples have "control" issues, not just Myron and me. "It's a male-female thing," I thought. How normal.

Recently I was at a village fair and Myron and I were sitting at a long table eating our clam cakes and Rhode Island "chowda". Three women about my age sat at the table near us. The entire time we were trying to enjoy our lunch I could hear these nicely dressed ladies gossip about another woman whom they all knew.

"She really shouldn't have gone out to the night club that night without her husband."

"Well, I don't think she knows what she is doing half the time, anyway, even if she was with friends from work."

"I'm glad I'm not her husband."

I thought, "How mean."

Another time in the grocery store I heard a mother shout at her two small children that they were going to "get it" when they got home if they didn't behave. I overheard another lady walking along the shore at the beach one afternoon speaking on her cell phone. It was trivial talk about what color her daughter-in-law's kitchen was and how it should have been painted in another color. Why not enjoy the beautiful view at the beach instead of talking publicly on the phone about such trite matters?

I notice that people scream at each other. Another day at the beach I was appalled to see a young mother stand on a pile of rocks way across the beach from her children and continue to yell at each child one at a time to "get out of the water right now" or there would be hell to pay later. It would have been so much easier to walk over to the children and talk to them quietly instead of letting the whole beach know what a tyrant she was. I was embarrassed for this woman. These are new lessons for me to hear what folks are saying "out there" in the big bad world. My upbringing and my inability to hear sheltered me from that world. I guess I really have been living in my own little rose-colored "Sound of Music" world, as my daughter, Sharon says.

When I listen to the radio I do not listen to the AM stations where listeners call in to complain about the government, politics and public figures. I listen to National Public Radio on FM which I enjoy for the most part. I like the interviews with experts from around the country. I enjoy the writers' interviews and hearing what they have to say about what they have written. After a while, when I realize that the focus is too centered on details about wars, I find myself changing the channel. I know the wars are there but I can't do much about them, so the continuous reporting live from distant lands becomes unsettling as I am not used to hearing about that kind of thing all the time.

Now I can hear my neighbors and I wonder if that is always a good thing. In the past I was not aware of children screaming so much in their play and adults making more noise as their parties continued into the night. Perhaps it was a delight to watch the children play and not hear them arguing with each other or fighting over toys they wanted to use. In summer I am privy to the water play and the accompanying screaming and yelling and sometimes crying when someone is hurt. When spending time with some of my grandchildren I can now hear when they occasionally criticize and say mean things to each other. I may have missed a lot of that in my childhood. I do remember not feeling comfortable sitting around in circles eating lunch because I couldn't keep up with the "girl talk" and gossip. And I know that I hated cafeteria at lunch in junior high school. It must have been because I couldn't hear what was going on around me.

So it seems that the hearing world is not all roses and I have some new things to hear and get used to. This does not mean that I am going to become cynical and rude to others as many seem to do. If anything, it strengthens my resolve to spread the "*Tea with Marie*" concepts of beauty, gentility and tranquility. Now that I hear so much better I am more equipped with the tools I need to continue this mission. As one friend says, I am "in a hallway between closed doors" in my life now. I know that I will proceed to another project or mission. Learning about what I never thought I'd hear will help me to understand about what new pathways to follow.

Someone asked me recently what I did not like about hearing with my new cochlear implant.

"I never knew the world around me was so noisy," was the first thing that popped into my mind.

Shortly after my new implant activation, I was shopping in one of my favorite department stores and trying on dresses in the fitting rooms when I became aware of the Muzak bothering my ears. I had never been aware of it before as I couldn't hear it. Now it was starting to drum away in my head and I was getting a headache. I had to finish up and get out of there quickly. Another example is the theater at intermission. The noise is thundering as people compete to shout over each other's voices. On city streets the cars, trucks and buses sound so loud also. I hear the neighbors, their arguments and their little kids screaming as they are playing outside. It used to be so quiet in my neighborhood before. I now hear lawn mowers on Sunday mornings and wood-splitting machines on holidays.

A few years back another person with a sense of curiosity and a lack of tact asked me what it was like to be deaf.

"Surely it must be so awful," she said.

"Well," I replied "not always."

Then I remembered how nice it was to wake up silently in the morning and not put my hearing aids in right away. I could drink my tea or coffee, eat breakfast quietly and notice my surroundings, such as the winter light playing on the colors of the carpet or (when I drank my coffee on the deck in the summer) the boldness of the hues of the flowers in my garden. Then, after I had taken my shower and dressed, I could put in my aids and join the world of sound. Since I have had that habit for so long I still find myself relishing the early moments of silence before putting on my processor to enter the real world. Lately my husband and I are both engaging in this habit of greeting the day silently with the captioning on the television or the newspaper in front of us. It is really like a form of meditation to greet the busy day in silence before rushing off to our various duties. So, in that regard, being deaf is a kind of a respite and a small "vacation" from the worldly noises.

If you want to simulate the feeling of being deaf and not hearing, put ear plugs on, watch the television with the mute button or go into a deep dark cave and listen to the sound of silence there in the empty dark void. When I used to teach workshops, especially those in schools, I would have some of the students wear ear plugs during the classes and then talk about how they felt at the end of the class and how much they were able to understand. Some said that they started to unconsciously watch faces and try to read lips. Others felt lonely and isolated and still others felt very uncomfortable, ill at ease and even scared.

So it seems that we are uncomfortable with silence in our busy world. And yet I think that it could be helpful to us to engage in quiet contemplation once or twice a day to help balance our lives and stay healthy and not become run down or stressed out. This is part of the premise behind my show, "Tea with Marie." I chose the tea ceremony as the metaphor but it could be yoga, tai chi, music or art. We need time to slow down and be silent as we listen to our inner soul or spirit and learn to appreciate our lives in the moment. This makes our lives so much more satisfying. Also, when we are at peace or feel calm we are better able to relate to people around us.

There are gifts in all things that happen to us. Opportunities to learn surround us and occur all the time. Life is full of changes, and we need to be flexible and open to rolling with the tide instead of fighting it, no matter what the circumstances. So it is with the matter of hearing. In the silence we can appreciate the stillness of the earth and the peace in our lives that can help us find balance and tranquility. All of us should leave some room for silence in our lives.

25

Our Cochlear Implant Group

June 2008

I have a friend named Nancy Shuster. We met when she came to one of my hearing technology workshops at a local library a few years ago. She was hard of hearing and wanted to learn more about technology to help herself communicate. After the program she gave me her card. One thing led to another. I realized that she was a writer's consultant. I told Nancy that I was thinking of writing a book but not sure about what to write. Nancy suggested that I write a book about hearing loss but I wanted to put together a collection of some columns I had written for "The South County Independent." Nancy and I met and she helped me to focus on the book that I wrote in 2003, called *"Simply South County."* Nancy decided to write a small book about hearing loss called *"Hearing Loss and Winning Solutions."* The following summer we helped each other edit our new books.

A couple of years ago Nancy woke up one morning and was stone deaf in each ear. The doctors had no idea why. It was a very difficult time for Nancy as you can well imagine. She had to use a paper and pencil to communicate with her family and others. Nancy is a very outgoing person, so this was especially hard for her. Nancy is also a smart person who likes to stay on top of things. The year before she had done a lot of research about the cochlear implant, so she was ready to call the University of Massachusetts Memorial Hospital in Worcester. After researching many places in New England, Nancy found that she was most satisfied with Dr. Daniel Lee at UMass Memorial. She called them right away and asked to sign up for an appointment for surgery. Nancy had her surgery and it was incredibly successful. Nancy is seventy some years old and she was able to hear clearly right away as soon as she was activated, which is very unusual. This may have had something to do with the fact that she had not been deaf that long and her brain had recent memories of hearing so it could get right back to stimulating the nerves again. Because of Nancy's extensive research, I could quickly move forward with my own plans for surgery. I also choose Dr. Lee at UMass Memorial.

This example illustrates how important it is for one to have support from others when pursuing such an important procedure as surgery. Last summer Nancy and some others in our town started a group with people who have cochlear implants or those who were interested in implants. Nancy got the ball rolling by starting the group and we all helped.

Nancy has a reputation for starting groups wherever she goes. She spends her year in three different places, Florida in winter, Providence in the fall and Narragansett in the summer, so she has started many groups.

We had several meetings last summer and then we decided to continue when Nancy came back in the late spring. We meet in our town library which lets us have the room once a month. We take turns organizing the group which means planning a topic, putting notices in the paper and contacting the members. Our early group meetings centered on getting to know each other, networking and sharing experiences. The implant users had much to say and share with each other. It felt good to learn helpful new information or to be able to share information with others. There was an interest in our small town and we had a good-sized group attend our meetings.

Our most recent meeting this year was very successful and we had thirteen people present. The room was small so we sat around a table where we could see and hear each other better. On one side of the room sat the majority of the guests who had received cochlear implants in the past few years. They were males and females of various ages from fifties to eighty-something. On the other side of the room sat several very nervous and strained looking adults who could not hear well at all and were having great difficulty just following the conversation going around the room (although we tried to speak one at a time and be considerate of their needs). There was also a professional present who had much information to share about resources for hard-of-hearing folks in our state such as specialized telephones, assistive listening and alerting devices.

There was time for sharing and going around the circle to introduce ourselves and state why we were there. The cochlear implant folks seemed happy and at ease understanding the conversation in contrast to the severe to profound hearing loss guests who were so obviously struggling. These folks shared their angst and their daily frustrations.

"I can't hear anything in this group."

"My children don't understand what I need."

"I feel left out of family conversations."

"I dread the holidays coming up."

"My wife says I keep the television on too loud."

"My husband keeps the television on too loud."

"Is there anything that can help me?"

Of course, we could all relate as we were there a few years ago. With patience, communication started flowing back and forth across the table. Stories were told, names and e-mails exchanged and encouraging advice was shared among the group members. Denise, our professional, had a vast source of worthwhile information available. At the end of the meeting, the hard-of-hearing folks seemed more relaxed as they expressed how much they had been helped. This can happen in any kind of support group where you feel alone and need to know that others are in the same place and are ready to help. We ended our meeting on a bright note and decided who would lead the meetings coming up. I will lead one coming up in a few months and have suggested that we bring our spouses or significant others to that meeting so that we can share worth-while strategies that work in relationships or vent our frustrations together. Everyone seemed to think this was a good idea. So if you have a big issue or an illness and want to get some help and support just think about starting a group as my friend Nancy does, and you may find the experience both worthwhile and enjoyable.

26

What I learned From France

July 2008

I have been to various places in France as well as to Paris a few times over the years as I love France and also have family there. But those were the days when I could not hear as well as I do now with my implant so I was looking forward to going with Myron this summer to my nephew, Hervé's wedding, in Chambéry, in the Alps. I was eager to also see how my implant would help with my French. I was not disappointed. In fact I spent more than a week speaking French every day with my relatives and to all the merchants, fellow travelers and other French people that I met. At the beginning of our vacation, French people would return my French attempts with their limited English, but by the end of the week I had a few who actually thought I was French! I was thrilled. It is not that when you get an implant you suddenly start speaking French, as we joked about in my family, but that when you hear better you can improve your language skills or anything else that you want to do or learn.

Since I have returned I have been asking myself what it was that I enjoyed so much about France and why it was so hard to leave. Many of the things I liked fit right in with my "Tea with Marie" philosophy of beauty, gentility and tranquility. Take tranquility, for example. We found that in our planning for the day we had to get out early to our destination so we could visit places in the morning as everything would be closed between 12 noon and 2 p.m. except for restaurants and cafes. The noon-day meal is one taken with leisure and not rushed through to get back to the office. We saw many working people sitting in the parks or near the lakes reading or relaxing after their lunch. This was a tranquil time before they had to return to work for 2 p.m. How nice to not be rushed in the middle of the work day and to have a chance to regroup.

I noticed that when you walked into a shop or even up to the cashier in the supermarket you heard a "Bonjour, Madame" and an "Au revoir, Madame" as you left and you were expected to respond to these greetings. Does this not make you feel like a human being and not just a hurried customer as the cashiers push your food along the conveyer belt? In fact, everywhere you go people greet you as a general rule. In the mornings my family members always ask each other if they have slept well. Then there are the ubiquitous kisses on both cheeks when relatives and friends greet each other. It is nice to have manners and to be polite and gracious to each other. It makes the world around you more pleasant.

The meals, ah the cuisine! It is not a simple thing in France. Many families still eat their main dinner in the middle of the day and have a light supper at night. But first we started our day with those delicious flaky croissants (that are not quite the same here) and fresh tasting butter and jam in the sunny breakfast room of the inn. There I could practice my French on the staff and the visitors from England, Austria and France (as well as speak English or a little German). I think it was just the concept of being able to share bread with visitors from countries of different languages and customs that excited me each morning. Many times at noon my cousin made us a complete dinner with four or five courses, including the local wines and cheeses (we were in Savoie in the Alps-Rhone region). Everyone, including the little eight-year-old boy, Dylan, sat for at least an hour or more and enjoyed the food and conversation. There was no technology or other stimulation available to distract. We ate outside and it was satisfying enough to enjoy the sensuality of the smells and flavors of the food and the companionship of your family members. It was a most pleasant form of connecting. I wonder how many of us still sit down to dinner with our families today in the United States squeezed in between all of our busy activities.

We attended the wedding of my nephew and it was more of a community affair. The day before the event, family and close friends drove up to the top of the mountain in the stifling heat and helped to prepare the hall with drapes and decorations and some of the kitchen preparations before the actual caterer would arrive for the wedding itself. On the day of the wedding everyone went first to the town hall for the civil service where the mayor led the ceremony. Then we drove in cavalcade, following the bridal limousine, an antique Rolls Royce that belonged to a close friend, to the church at the top of a mountain for the religious service. I enjoyed saying the Lord's Prayer (Notre Pére) in French with everyone. There were many similar customs even though the wedding was in France and not Rhode Island. Afterwards, the reception took place in the hall ("salle") across the street from the church that had been decorated in the theme colors of brown and white the day before by family and friends. The food started with a long table of what was billed as "Buffet d'entrées" and included a large, colorful and attractively presented selection of appetizers and Hors d'oeuvres done with a French flair. Then there was "Filet de Boêuf en croute sauce forestière" with several vegetable accompaniments for the main course. The large cheese cart filled with cheeses from all over France was my favorite. I knew that it would be a long time before I would encounter such a delectable assortment of fine French cheeses. The day after the wedding the group of family and friends returned to the hall to clean up and enjoy another delicious meal of the leftovers that was spread out elegantly, a "second wedding" and another opportunity for family and close friends to share and have fun together.

I couldn't help admiring the ways we observed in Europe that energy was conserved and the environment was protected and valued. Public places we visited along the lakes and in the parks in Switzerland and France had bins for recycling trash. Most public areas and streets were clean and not filled with rubbish. Colorful flowers brightening window boxes on houses and in public squares were everywhere. Fountains and benches were available for people to sit and relax in the parks. And of course there were small cars that were more practical with the high prices of gasoline and the need for conservation. I also noticed that bike paths were not exclusively for recreational use but were located in cities where we watched commuters actually riding their bikes to work. We saw many vegetable gardens in the yards of homeowners who depended on the fresh produce for their meals. This concept of "Victory Gardens" had been popular during the wars in Europe.

Because I had a bad heat rash while in France I was able to witness some aspects of their medical system. We went to pharmacies, which were smaller and less cluttered and where the pharmacist was readily available behind the counter facing the entrance. They were not hidden behind a glass case in the back of some large box store. One pharmacist gave me some helpful advice regarding creams and medicine for my rash. Because my rash was still not clearing I had to visit my cousin's doctor. There Myron and I were pleased to witness the relative simplicity of the arrangement in his office. The doctor consulted with us at his desk, took my blood pressure and did a thorough examination on the table in another area of his office. Then the doctor returned to the desk to give us diagnosis and collect the fee. There was no extra staff except for a shared receptionist in the hall. Myron also noticed that the doctor had house calls listed on his fee chart! My prescriptions were inexpensive and the whole prescription paper process was much simpler than ours.

Throughout our travels I was able to help Myron by responding to questions, travel directions and challenges in the airports and on the highway. This was not only because I could speak French but because I could hear so much better. It was the first time we had traveled to Europe after I had my implant. My confidence grew as I took care of situations that arose by conversing in French and handling problems that arose. I felt comfortable in Europe where life seemed slower and people more appreciative of simple things. I was glad to have the opportunity to be there again, participating in their customs, learning new things and enjoying the people and the beautiful scenery.

27

"Communi'tea" At The Farm

July 2008

We have a farmer's market up the road that meets on Saturday mornings in the summer time. It has been going on for the past few years and is run by a cooperative at the historic Casey Farm. Casey Farm is really an old "Yankee plantation" that was built in New England during the eighteenth century. It is designated to be preserved and operated as an historic farm. It is enjoyable to drive by the farm on the old Boston Neck Road by car or by bike, leaving the twenty-first century for a few seconds as you view the old farm house and catch the bucolic smells in the fields. The two story square white farmhouse faces south overlooking grounds that are surrounded by stone walls and cooperatively cultivated fields of vegetables. To the north and east are barns and coops filled with Rhode Island Red chickens and more fields with sheep, cows and horses that wander through the grasses that slope downward toward Narragansett Bay. Across the bay is the island of Jamestown and on the other side of Jamestown is Newport. Locals and tourists alike, slow down to enjoy the view when they drive through this portion of the road through Saunderstown, whether on their way to amusements in Newport or nearby to do errands.

On summer Saturday mornings organic vendors from around Rhode Island arrive at Casey Farm to pitch their raw oysters and lobsters from local waters, artisan breads, large varieties of farm vegetables and produce, fresh cut flowers, beef and dairy products. On a clear day the walled lot devoted to parking is filled with Toyota Priuses, trucks and other vehicles as folks file out through the stone walls up to the field where the vendors are located. Denim overall-ed men and women with floppy straw hats and gentle smiles stand behind their booths to explain about their homegrown honey or cheese while proffering samples for you to taste. The vendors surround a field that leaves enough room for friends to congregate, chat and connect with each other. Sometimes "Doc" Wood will be there, strumming his banjo and singing folk songs under the shade tree at the end of the field where an appreciative crowd gathers. "Doc" and his wife, Judy, are also award-winning photographers in the community.

This particular Saturday in July was sunny and warm with a gentle breeze and not hot and humid as it can be at this time. I meandered through the field, keeping an eye out for some rosemary plants to add to my herb collection. Then I spotted the most heavenly soft red freshly picked raspberries in boxes on a table. After purchasing the raspberries and depositing the box in my grandchild's orange plastic beach pail (the only container I had available in my car) I turned around and nearly bumped into my friends, Eileen and Capers. Eileen had received her cochlear implant about five years ago and she was my chief support as I went through the procedure last year. Eileen has started a non-profit foundation called "The Gift of Hearing" in order to aid deaf children and others who can't afford the implants. We stopped and caught up on a little business about our local cochlear implant group that meets once a month.

As I walked toward another booth I saw a young woman from my church named Erin, who explained to me about the sermon she would be giving next month. She mentioned that the theme would be about how we need a "village" or a community in our lives to help us survive in many ways. Erin is a young mother who has organized a unique support community for mothers and children. Our church, the Unitarian Universalist congregation here in South County, certainly provides a community for Myron and myself, whose children are grown. We enjoy coming together weekly to meet spiritually and connect with caring friends. At the moment, Myron is working hard to make sure our new church building is environmentally and ergonomically friendly for those with hearing loss. We will be moving into a new location and we want our church community to be accessible to all. I am involved as the hospitality chairwoman at our church.

While leaving the farmer's coop market and about to pull out of the lot I beeped my horn at a couple that was passing in front of my car. They were Dave and Deb, quite coincidentally another couple that goes to our church. Dave is helping Myron with the hearing accessibility project and mentioned an idea he had for it. After exchanging a few more thoughts, smiles and ideas we took leave of each other.

I drove home but not without feeling totally content. It was an outstanding summer day, the sky was blue, the clouds drifting by and I was headed home to sample the fresh raspberries and "play" in my flower garden. I felt grateful for this Saturday morning opportunity to "take tea" as I call it in my basket of metaphors. For me, that means an opportunity to connect just as one enjoys tea with friends or loved ones. This time it was a connection in our community with friends at the market "communi'tea". Like my friend, Erin, I find that the communities around us are important to help us feel truly human. I believe that it is when we join together peacefully in groups with others that we discover that most people deep down are really just like us with their pains, sorrows, joys and happiness that are a part of living. Connecting with others promotes strength and feelings of warmth within that help us continue through the ups and downs of life.

28

Fear Of Teaching And New York

November 2008

The kids lost me in the Norman Bird Sanctuary in 1984. The kids I am talking about were the seventh-graders in my science class. It was a field trip and the class and I were walking through the woods in the sanctuary looking for wildlife and enjoying being out of doors away from the classroom in spring when someone got the bright idea that it might be fun to play a trick on the hard-of-hearing teacher. Suddenly I found myself rushing through the nature preserve trying to find fifteen preteens who were my responsibility. As I raced through the woods in a state of agitation all I could think of was that my own two kids were home waiting for me to take them to the orthodontist and I was here after school hours, trying to find some kids whose idea of a joke was to drive their teacher nuts. The headmaster was called, the kids were eventually found and I went home late to my family feeling mortified, embarrassed and hurt.

This was the episode that made me decide against continuing my teaching career. By the end of that year I gave up teaching and tried to figure out what I was going to do the rest of my life to support my children and myself. I was greatly affected by the incident and even more torn by the fact that my hearing was worsening and I didn't know what I was going to do next to survive. Eventually I got over that hurdle and moved on with my life. Teaching had been a challenge for me, as I struggled every day to listen to the kids in the classroom and then collapsed on the couch from exhaustion after getting home every night. I loved the concept of teaching and helping children learn but I was limited by my physical capabilities.

New York was incredibly noisy when Myron and I went there during the winter on our annual Santa Claus trips on the holiday train. It was hard on our hearing aids as the background noise of cars, cabs and trucks would overwhelm us. Inevitably, Myron and I would start arguing as we sloshed through the snow and ice in the harsh wind and cold trying to find our way around the city. It was hard to tell where the noises were coming from and to avoid being run over by fast taxis and cars that we couldn't hear coming. Myron would become disoriented and I would be left trying to find the way and deal with his confusion as well as my own. I really didn't like going to New York any more. That was too bad because one of the things I enjoyed while growing up in New Jersey was going into Manhattan to a play or shopping or visiting Rockefeller Center. It had now actually become frightening for me to go to New York and I stopped going on the holiday trips because they were too stressful.

This year my battles with both teaching and New York were finally over. After my implant I began to hear so much better, not perfectly, like normal hearing people, but probably more like someone with a moderate loss. It felt good enough for me however, as I was doing fine so I had my teaching certificates updated after not having used them for twenty-five years. I registered to substitute teach in a couple of towns and waited for the phone to ring. My first call came at eight o'clock and they asked if I could get to the elementary school by nine o'clock. I said, "Yes," quickly showered, dressed and then hurried down the highway to the school. It had been twenty-five years since my last experience teaching yet the burdensome feelings from the past were coming to the surface and I felt nervous and jittery. How did I know I could do it this time?

The attractive, efficient, young principal walked me to the classroom and explained a little about the class. An aide was reading to the seventeen children when I arrived in the room. It was time for the aide to leave. Now I was alone looking down at these seventeen sweet little faces sitting on the rug that were entirely my responsibility for the whole day. Inside I was a nervous wreck and wanted to panic, but I said to myself, "OK, you must stay calm on the outside for the children." There had been no time to read the substitute guide. I had no idea what the methods were this school used to keep order in the classroom. On the desk was a stack of directions left from the teacher and in front of me were the little faces, with short attention spans, I imagined.

Earlier I had heard someone mention that there had been a fire at the school yesterday. "Oh, dear," I thought, "This was the elementary school with the fire that was on the news last night." So my family therapist background re-emerged and I decided that these kids needed a chance to talk about and "process" the fire. The children raised their hands and were glad to explain the many features of the story of the fire to me. Then I looked down in front of me to a face I hadn't seen and this small boy sat there with tears running down his face.

"I want to, want to, talk about, about, the fire," his tiny voice whispered as I asked him to repeat what he said. When I heard what he said the second time I assured him that he would also have a turn to tell us about the fire.

Then, with the assistance of another boy, who was being so helpful (I believe he thought he was the teacher himself), that I realized we were supposed to be completing a lesson about letters on the board. I thanked him for his help and referred to the teacher's plan as I introduced the lesson. To keep the children's attention I resorted to adding a little sign language lesson into the mix. So far I could hear the little voices. Good. I was not used to teaching the little ones as most of my experience had been with middle-schoolers and high school students. I was hanging in there. Soon we had a few more lessons and it was time to take the children to recess and lunch. As we walked down the hallway I felt a tiny hand in mine from a sweet little boy with no hair on his head and a darling smile on his face.

After lunch the music teacher came for the kids and I had time to read the lesson plans and the substitute guide. The nurse called me to tell me about the child with the peanut allergy and to be sure to check all the snacks of the kids. Eventually it was time to make sure the kids got on the right school bus in the fleet of six buses assigned to this class alone. While rounding up the children I heard a few "Are you coming again?" and then I felt some goodbye hugs. I smiled. The kids all made it to their buses with the help of some fifth-graders and I said "Goodbye" and was able to breathe. The children and I had made it through my first day back to teaching and all of us had survived.

As for New York, I had an opportunity to visit with a friend of mine at a writer's conference. I enjoyed the gorgeous fall scenery of brilliant colors and the glistening water along the coastal Connecticut countryside on the train ride into the city. My stomach was churning nastily. My friend, Pat, was chattering about what our intentions would be for the conference. It was hard for me to get in the spirit. I explained to her what we would have to do when we reached Penn Station as she was not familiar with the city. When we arrived and stepped out into the street, pulling our rolling bags behind us, I noticed the city noise but I also noticed that it was bearable! No more throbbing hearing aids and I didn't start to get a headache. My processor seemed to be handling this noisy environment with aplomb. I told Pat which direction we needed to follow to find our hotel. With each step on our walk I felt more confident.

That weekend Pat and I stood in line at the Empire State building for an hour and a half, went out to eat in noisy restaurants where I could hear her talking to me and enjoyed the programs of the two day conference on Park Avenue. After a day, I was the one leading Pat and some other participants around town with no fear. I was able to hear all the speakers at the conference, asked a few questions in front of the large audience and had many opportunities to chat with writers from around the country. I faced one of the well known agents after standing in line for an hour and enthusiastically explained to her about my project. She said to send her my proposal. I learned so much from so many at the conference. It was exhilarating to "blend in" with the crowd, enjoy luncheon conversations, share information and not worry about who was saying what and whether I could hear. My hearing was better and my confidence was building. Walking through the streets of New York City evolved into a welcoming experience for me and I let myself get caught up in the excitement of the city, the crowds and even the city noises.

29

I Hear The Birds

October 2008

As a child I used to spend time during the summer in Sag Harbor with my grandmother, whom I called "Dearie." My mother was also there as well as my sister, grandfather and sometimes my father, but the one I seemed to enjoy being with the most was my eighty-year-old grandmother. In the mornings I couldn't wait to wake up, race down the stairs and run into my grandmother's bedroom on the first floor where she was lying in her high antique bed. I would climb up on the bed and land in my grandmother's arms for a hug and a "Bonjour, Ma Cherie." I always responded "Bonjour Ma Cherie". Those were the first words of French that I learned. Then Dearie might invite me to enjoy samples off her breakfast tray that Margaret had brought for her, such as nibbles of toast or tastes of oatmeal. Dearie and I would have the most wonderful conversations. I always listened carefully as she explained to me about what she had read in the Times that morning. It might have been stories about the brave General Eisenhower or the charismatic young minister, Billy Graham.

Sometimes Dearie and I would look out the windows in front of her bed and search for some of the birds. Dearie had this little black book with the birds and descriptions of their habitats and characteristics. We would pore over the book together as she told me about the catbirds, Baltimore orioles and whip-poor-wills. These were the first birds I heard about. I remember that Dearie used to talk about the different songs of the birds but I can't remember hearing those songs. Reading together from the little book about the birds made them seem as though they were Dearie's and my own special friends.

My own children also had the privilege of spending summers at Sagabon and building many memories with my mother, their grandmother. When we went to the country to visit we would all look forward to the special times that my mother would provide. My father had died when Joy was a baby so it was my mother whom my children remember. Mother would have the place as clean as a whistle, "Sagabon" soup with tomatoes, celery and ham stock simmering on the stove and the nursery filled with stuffed animals and toys in the various cribs and beds for the kids. The house was surrounded by meadows, woods and ponds and beaches were a short walk down the sandy lane. The kids loved to explore and would come back with wild flowers or tortoises they kept for a little while before returning them to their natural habitats. At Christmas the eighteenth-century farmhouse was filled with holly and pine greens from the property, and my mother would outdo herself with the food and holiday preparations.

Summer at Sagabon revolved around the gardens. One of the responsibilities that belonged to my young son was to refill the bird baths, bird feeders and suet holders. In the mornings, Tommy would wake up earlier than the rest of us and rush down to my mother in the kitchen, where he and she would watch eagerly at the back door for the various birds and the pheasants and quail that came walking up the meadow. Mom helped Tom learn the names of the birds. Soon my son became an amateur ornithologist and he has kept this interest all his life. Tom now shares this passion with his own children, my grandchildren. So the family legacy continues. I have been birding with Tom in many refuges, and he has been able to point out the camouflaged birds hidden in the trees and bushes as well as recognize their individual songs when I did not even know the birds were singing.

In my own garden I always feed the birds and enjoy watching them. In front of the kitchen window over the sink I have placed a feeder so I can gaze at the birds while doing the dishes. For several years we had a bird house on one of our trees where sparrows would return to nest. I look forward to the goldfinches' return in spring and the chickadees playing during the winter. The nuthatches, purple finches and cardinals add more variety to our yard. The birds have always played an integral part of my garden. Every year I look forward to spring to get out in the earth and to start building new creations of color in my "outdoor" rooms. The time I would spend in my garden would be silent and since I did not know differently I would not miss anything. I took pleasure in the visual beauty and the solitude and tranquility of the garden. After a while I would lose time in my garden and forget to come in to make supper.

This past year the pre-summer days were particularly lovely. Mornings I spent doing the usual things such as exercise, picking up the house, catching up on paperwork or other tasks. After lunch I would enjoy sitting in the sun outside on the deck in the garden for a while. My simple yard has actually converted into a real garden over the years here in Narragansett. Each year I discover a new project to enhance the garden and I am constantly transplanting. It will never be Sagabon but it has become my own little sanctuary. I love the garden in May and June when the beds are starting to fill in, the lawn looks decent and the lilacs and azaleas are blooming. The parade of dominating yellows of forsythia, narcissus and daffodils has given way to the purples and lavenders of myrtle, violets, lilacs and waves of Japanese iris. Then the delight of the fragrant, old-fashioned roses arrives.

One dazzling sunny day last June, about a week after my cochlear implant activation, I felt strong enough to go outside into the garden. I started to walk very slowly around the yard enjoying the smells and colors of spring. I heard some strange chirping sounds so I stood still in my backyard and listened carefully.

"What could that be?" I thought, as I remained quietly mesmerized for a few minutes. I hadn't expected to hear anything. Then I looked up and saw some birds flying by. It took me a couple of seconds to make the connection.

"Oh, no, those are the songs of the birds in my garden! How amazing!" To be able to see and hear them was a blessing. I stood in my backyard as tears rolled down my cheeks. I had not heard birds for forty years. How can you know what you are missing when you are missing it? Memories of my grand-mother, Dearie, came floating fuzzily in my head. The connection I felt when lying on Dearie's bed watching the birds with her was engulfed in the new feelings I was experiencing. Connection, I thought. A deeper level of connection was mak-ing itself available to me. Perhaps now I would be able to hear those songs of the whip-poor-will that Dearie described. Per-haps now I could go birding with my son and learn to recognize the various warblers' songs. That afternoon I spent several hours by myself, lying in the warm sun on a lounge chair, listening to the sweet songs of the birds whom I had enjoyed watching for so many years but whom I was finally able to hear again.

Not hearing is knowing the birds are there but not being able to fully appreciate them because you can't hear them sing. Not hearing is being in a silent bubble looking out at the world. It is watching television with the sound turned off. It is walking into a pitch black underground cave where silence can be sliced like a piece of pie. Hearing is knowing someone is behind you when they say "Good morning." It is moving out of the way when someone says, "Excuse me." It is jumping quickly away when a car is coming toward you. Hearing is knowing your baby upstairs is crying. Hearing is listening to the opera on a sunny Saturday afternoon. Hearing is opening the door of your world of silence to a greater dimension that includes joy and sadness. Hearing is having more opportunities. To hear the birds sing is to fully appreciate the world around you.

30

What's Next?

August 2008

The past year has been an amazing journey and the excitement still continues. Almost every day I discover a new opportunity to hear something that I was not able to hear before my operation. A few days ago we went to the theater and saw "The Producers." I was sitting there listening to everything when I suddenly stopped myself short. "Oh, my goodness I AM listening to everything," I thought to myself. I can actually hear the actors, their dialogue and most of the lyrics of the songs. I used to only be able to watch the colorful scenery and dancing and listen to the melodies of the music from the orchestra when I went to the theater. I looked over at Myron by my side and felt bad for him as I knew he could hear none of it and that was the way I used to be.

So what happens next with this gift that has been given to me? I have been thinking about this. Women, especially, reach many crossroads during their lives. This is another one of mine. I knew I would finish this book before I started another project, but what would it be? I know that my hearing has changed and my means of communicating are much better but I wonder if my basic core values have changed. I don't think so. I still believe in the premises behind my show, "*Tea with Marie.*" I can see and hear that many people are so busy today they can't find time to slow down and include more beauty in their lives. Children are also continually scheduled so that they can't learn about including the tranquility that will ultimately lead them to healthier and more balanced lives as they grow older. Beauty is found in many forms such as in art, music, dance and literature. It is also found in thoughtful and considerate gestures we make for ourselves and towards others. I believe that we need to add elements to our lives to make them more refined and gentle.

I, too, have been a victim of multitasking, over scheduling and being pulled in all directions without stopping. Then I had my implant operation and was forced to rest for about four weeks. The first week was difficult. I wanted to be up and about as I was so bored. But soon I started to enjoy the leisurely schedule and the afternoon nap. This helped to put relaxation back into my life each day and to really examine how I said "yes" to others. I am more circumspect now and plan my time doing what is better for me (and therefore better for those around me.) And of course I need my cup of tea around four o'clock to calm my spirits and renew my energy. As my grandmother used to say, "I cannot live without my afternoon cup of tea." Is this not a way of putting beauty in your life and the lives of those near and dear to you?

When I can hear more around me I can see that the world is not always a happy place. My rose-colored life is being affected by new information and input to my brain. I see a lot of anger in the world and I hear about it on the radio and television. I observe impatience and rudeness in people and a lack of consideration. This just strengthens my resolve to want to do something about this incivility. I need to continue my own ways of including tranquility in my life. It is important for all of us to connect with ourselves on a regular basis or we can start to lose touch and risk becoming ill and unhappy.

Taking time to prepare for an annual holiday tea gives us a chance to put more beauty in our lives. You attend to the details and it is like preparing a gift for your friends and those you hold dear. Then you bring your guests together and when you see them enjoying themselves you feel peaceful. You are gathering your guests to help them stop, slow down, take the time to have tea and connect with each other during the hectic holiday season. This is really what the holidays are all about, not dashing from store to store with a ridiculously long list you are trying to fill as you spend all your money. My special friends, the "tea ladies," and I once held a tea for middle-schoolers at a local inn solely for the purpose of honoring these adolescents. We hoped to help the girls learn that there are times you have to do something special for yourself. For them it was a break from their busy lives and a chance to learn about etiquette in a lovely atmosphere. I still hear from some of these girls about how they never forgot that special day.

Many stress "living in the moment" today as the healthiest way to live. And, why not? Because it makes sense. If you appreciate and fully participate in the life surrounding you with all your senses you are truly feeling alive. I have found that my past includes many mistakes that I made and things I wish I had done differently. I wish that I had been more mature as a parent and had made better decisions as a wife. But there is nothing that you can do about your past and you are not in control of your future so it is wise not to focus on them all the time. Live in the moment and enjoy the beauty of life. Take time for some tranquility and perhaps a cup of tea or another ritual that promotes peace and balance in your life. If you are doing things quietly and simply you are more apt to appreciate the beauty around you. We can do this whether we hear or don't hear, walk or don't walk and see or don't see.

I am grateful that I am able to hear more of the beautiful sounds around me in the world. I say this now being more aware of the ugliness that does exist. I never want to become so blasé that I take my hearing for granted. I have found that it is better to hear than not to hear and I have experienced both. Now that I have received this gift I think that I will probably want to use it for creative expression in my life to share some of my thoughts with others and to focus on the importance of living in beauty and tranquility. I am no longer the little girl whose mother protected and guided her. I have also grown as an adult woman in this past year. I am going to use my new-found confidence and ability to communicate by continuing to learn and create. Who knows, now that I can hear callers on the phone I may even start my own radio talk show with a positive focus during these challenging times. Perhaps I will call it "Pleasantly Positive" or "Positively Pleasant."

Toward the end of this year I found that it was time to let go of my award-winning cable television show, "Tea with Marie," after seven years of hosting and producing. It was becoming a challenge to gather together a volunteer crew every other week as well as other factors. I loved creating the show and working with my close friends and crew members but I had to do something healthy for myself by saying "no" and moving on. It was with mixed feelings, of course, and I do miss the show with the stimulation of meeting and learning from the guests. I know that I will find another worthwhile mission and I have faith in my creative future. This is what we must do for ourselves as I have found out time and time again. Life is a continuous series of extending and unfolding as we face the changes in our lives.

Afterword

Before Marie received her implant, we had spent two years doing research on the subject. That work took us to several hospitals and doctors' offices. We spent time speaking to cochlear implant recipients of all ages, their spouses and parents. Once we were convinced that Marie had a reasonable chance to hear music with a CI, she agreed to the procedure. We moved to the next step and sought out Dr. Daniel Lee to accept Marie as a patient for a cochlear implant.

Marie's concern about retaining the ability to hear music was put to rest. A few days after her activation (the placement and programming of the external processor) we attended an outdoor band concert. Marie cried during the opening National Anthem and every song thereafter. She was overjoyed as it was all wonderful music to her through her new digital ear. The complex sounds of music are no longer a challenge. She was fortunate enough to receive one of the first CI devices specifically designed for music.

More about Cochlear Implants is available on the Web. If you don't get too queasy watching medical videos, try YouTube.com. There are over 1800 videos on cochlear implant procedures and personal experiences.

Here are some websites of interest.
>   www.otosurgery.org/cochlearimplants.htm
>   www.edaud.org
>   www.ncbi.nlm.nih.gov/books/bv.fcgi?rid=hstat
>   www.shhh.org/
>   www.alda.org
>   www.hearinglossweb.com/
>   www.advancedbionics.com
>   www.cochlear.com/
>   www.medel.com/
>   www.giftofhearingfoundation.org

Myron Waldman

Biography

Marie Younkin-Waldman has been the recent host and producer for the Rhode Island award winning television show "Tea with Marie" for the past eight years. She has been a columnist with "The South County Independent" and "The Woman's Page" newspapers in Rhode Island. She is the author of *Simply South County*. Marie has undergraduate and graduate degrees from The American University in Paris and The University of Rhode Island. Her background is in education and she has taught from nursery school through high school. She is also a Marriage and Family Therapist. Marie worked in the field of disabilities for many years and served on various state councils as an advocate for hearing loss. She received a commendation from the State of Rhode Island for her work with the hearing impaired.

Myron Waldman is Marie's husband and they live in Narragansett, Rhode Island. She has four adult children (as does Myron) and seven grandchildren (as does Myron). Her hobbies include: gardening, birding, reading, decorating, biking, skiing, swimming and organizing charity teas. Marie has had a lifelong progressive bilateral sensory neural hearing loss. She recently underwent successful cochlear implant surgery on her right ear.

Marie's motto is:" Life is so exciting that I'll use whatever is necessary to enable me to participate in it!"

Speak with the Author on the Web

To continue the discussion, contact me through any of the following:

On Twitter at: **www.Twitter.com/teawithmarie**

On Facebook: **http://tinyurl.com/marie-on-facebook**

On my Website: **www.ToHearTheBirdsSing.com**

Where to Purchase On-line

www.Amazon.com

www.GentilityPress.com

31142461R00109

Made in the USA
Charleston, SC
07 July 2014